Estimates of Productivity Change by Industry

Estimates of Productivity Change by Industry

An Evaluation and an Alternative

Edward F. Denison

THE BROOKINGS INSTITUTION
WASHINGTON, D.C.

Library of Congress Cataloging-in-Publication Data

Denison, Edward Fulton, 1915–
Estimates of productivity change by industry : an evaluation and an alternative / Edward F. Denison.
p. cm.
Includes index.
ISBN 0-8157-1800-4 (alk. paper)
1. Industrial productivity—United States. 2. United States—Manufactures. 3. United States—Industries. I. Title.
HC110.I52D46 1989
338'.06'0973—dc19 88-26891
CIP

987654321

The paper used in this publication meets the minimum requirements of the American National Standard for Information Sciences—Permanence of Paper for Printed Library Materials, ANSI Z39.48-1984.

Set in Linotron Times Roman
Composition by Graphic Composition, Inc.,
Athens, Georgia
Printing by Bookcrafters
Chelsea, Michigan
Book design by Ken Sabol

THE BROOKINGS INSTITUTION

The Brookings Institution is an independent organization devoted to nonpartisan research, education, and publication in economics, government, foreign policy, and the social sciences generally. Its principal purposes are to aid in the development of sound public policies and to promote public understanding of issues of national importance.

The Institution was founded on December 8, 1927, to merge the activities of the Institute for Government Research, founded in 1916, the Institute of Economics, founded in 1922, and the Robert Brookings Graduate School of Economics and Government, founded in 1924.

The Board of Trustees is responsible for the general administration of the Institution, while the immediate direction of the policies, program, and staff is vested in the President, assisted by an advisory committee of the officers and staff. The by-laws of the Institution state: "It is the function of the Trustees to make possible the conduct of scientific research, and publication, under the most favorable conditions, and to safeguard the independence of the research staff in the pursuit of their studies and in the publication of the results of such studies. It is not a part of their function to determine, control, or influence the conduct of particular investigations or the conclusions reached."

The President bears final responsibility for the decision to publish a manuscript as a Brookings book. In reaching his judgment on the competence, accuracy, and objectivity of each study, the President is advised by the director of the appropriate research program and weighs the views of a panel of expert outside readers who report to him in confidence on the quality of the work. Publication of a work signifies that it is deemed a competent treatment worthy of public consideration but does not imply endorsement of conclusions or recommendations.

The Institution maintains its position of neutrality on issues of public policy in order to safeguard the intellectual freedom of the staff. Hence interpretations or conclusions in Brookings publications should be understood to be solely those of the authors and should not be attributed to the Institution, to its trustees, officers, or other staff members, or to the organizations that support its research.

FOREWORD

From 1948 to 1973 rates of productivity growth were the same in the manufacturing and nonmanufacturing portions of American business, according to government figures. The same data series show that in the 1980s productivity increased far less in nonmanufacturing industries than in manufacturing. This study questions whether such a drastic change has really occurred and casts doubt on the general reliability of these productivity series. It suggests that for productivity analysis classifying the business economy by final product rather than by industry would yield more accurate and meaningful information.

If indeed the division of productivity change between nonmanufacturing and manufacturing industries is inaccurate or misleading, there are implications for analyzing international competition as well as economic growth. Changes in unit labor costs in U.S. manufacturing are often compared with such changes in competitor nations. If, as the author concludes, the estimated increase in output per hour in U.S. manufacturing is not reliably estimated and is almost surely overstated, then the estimated rise in unit labor costs is also unreliable and is almost surely understated. Changes in the competitive position of American manufacturers are then somewhat less favorable than appear to be the case.

Edward F. Denison has been a senior fellow in the Brookings Economic Studies program since 1962 and is currently senior fellow emeritus. This study would not have been possible without the generous cooperation of the able government economists responsible for estimating U.S. productivity and the output measures entering into them. The author is especially grateful for information, comments, and suggestions from Robert P. Parker, associate director of the Bureau of

Economic Analysis; Jerome A. Mark, associate commissioner of the Bureau of Labor Statistics; and Edwin R. Dean, chief of the Division of Productivity Research at BLS. Jack Alterman, Frank de Leeuw, George Jaszi, Thomas K. Rymes, Jack E. Triplett, and Allan H. Young also provided valuable comments.

Caroline Lalire edited the manuscript, Victor M. Alfaro and Anna M. Nekoranec verified its factual content, and Florence Robinson prepared the index. E. Carole Hingleton, Valerie M. Owens, and Kathleen Elliott Yinug provided secretarial support. This book has been financed by funds of the Brookings Center for Economic Progress and Employment.

The views expressed here are those of the author and should not be ascribed to persons whose assistance is acknowledged above or to the trustees, officers, and other staff members of the Brookings Institution.

BRUCE K. MACLAURY
President

January 1989
Washington, D.C.

To George Jaszi
and
Charles F. Schwartz

CONTENTS

1. Introduction and Summary 1
Productivity Series and Their Characteristics 2
Measuring Production of Computers 8
Productivity by Industry 10
Productivity by End Product 13

2. The New Way of Measuring Production of Computers 15
Effect on the Growth of GNP and GNP per Hour 17
Effect on the Growth of NNP and NNP per Hour 21
The Weight for Computers in Output and Input 22
Inappropriateness of the New Computer Series to Measure Capital Input 24
Timing and Industry Distribution of Multifactor Productivity Change 32
Measurement of Computers and the Productivity Slowdown 35
The Computer and the Concept of Output Measurement 36
Conclusion 37

3. Estimates of Productivity by Industry 39
Growth Rates of Output per Hour by Industry 39
Ways of Estimating Output by Industry 42
Statistical Problems with the Output Estimates by Industry 44
Estimates of Hours of Work 56
Conclusion 58

4. Productivity by End Product: A Proposal 60
Conceptual Problems with Productivity by Industry 61
Direct Estimates of Productivity by End Product 64
Indirect Estimates of Productivity by End Product 68
Concluding Comment 74

Index 75

TABLES

1-1. Outcome per Hour in the Business Sector, Manufacturing and Nonmanufacturing, Amounts and Growth Rates, 1948–86 3

1-2. Annual Growth Rates of Multifactor Productivity in the Private Business Sector and Manufacturing, 1948–86 5

2-1. Effect of Exceptional Improvement in Output per Unit of Input in Computer Production on Growth Rates of Output per Hour in the Business Sector, Manufacturing and Nonmanufacturing, 1948–86 20

3-1. Annual Growth Rates of Output per Hour in the Business Sector, by Industry Group, 1948–86 40

3-2. 1982 Business Sector GNP Distributed by the Method Used to Estimate GNP in Constant Dollars by Industry 48

4-1. Growth Rates of Implicit Price Deflators and Differences in Implied Growth Rates of Output per Unit of Input for Gross Domestic Business Product and Its Final Product Components, 1929–86 70

Estimates of Productivity Change by Industry

chapter one

Introduction and Summary

In an effort to understand the slowdown in the growth of productivity in the United States since 1973, some observers have turned to estimates of productivity by industry. Their investigations have usually centered on industries within the business sector of the economy.[1]

Bureau of Labor Statistics (BLS) estimates show that from 1979 to 1986, when output per hour rose 1.4 percent a year in the business sector as a whole, it rose 3.5 percent in manufacturing industries and only 0.6 percent in nonmanufacturing industries. From 1982 to 1986 alone, a period of cyclical expansion, there was an even larger gap between the annual growth rates in manufacturing (5.0 percent) and nonmanufacturing (1.3 percent). The BLS series for multifactor productivity (defined shortly) imply similar differences between manufacturing and nonmanufacturing. A large difference in the growth rates of productivity between manufacturing and nonmanufacturing industries is a very recent development.

This study examines the statistical foundations for the reported growth rates of productivity by industry. I find that much of the recent manufacturing advantage stems from the extraordinary growth of measured productivity in computer production. This large effect is attributable to the overweighting of computers in total output and the debatable practice of assigning to the computer industry a huge increase in output based on improvements in the speed, versatility, and other characteristics of computers. At least part of the remaining difference between the measured growth of manufacturing and nonmanufacturing

1. The sector excludes employees of government (except government enterprises), nonprofit organizations, and private households and also the net inflow of income from abroad. The services either of all dwellings or (in the U.S. Bureau of Labor Statistics series) owner-occupied dwellings are also usually excluded for productivity analysis.

productivity seems to come from a methodology, imposed by inadequate information, that cannot partition the growth of national product among industries reliably and assigns too much of recent growth to manufacturing. Besides evaluating industry estimates, I urge an additional approach to disaggregation of productivity data—classification by end product as opposed to industry.

Productivity Series and Their Characteristics

The principal data I use in examining industry estimates are the BLS series for *output per hour* and *multifactor productivity* and the national accounts of the U.S. Bureau of Economic Analysis (BEA), from which the BLS data for output and, for the most part, capital stock are drawn.[2] The BLS measures output by gross national product (GNP), a measure that is gross of capital consumption (depreciation). The denominator for output per hour is the total number of hours that wage and salary workers were paid for and that self-employed persons and unpaid family workers worked. The denominator for multifactor productivity is a weighted average of the same series for hours and of series for the quantities of structures and equipment, inventories, and land used in production.[3]

Over the twenty-five years from 1948 through 1973 output per hour grew at about the same rate, 2.8 or 2.9 percent a year, in manufacturing, nonmanufacturing business, and the business sector as a whole (table 1-1). The sector growth rate then collapsed to 0.6 percent a year in 1973–79. Both manufacturing and nonmanufacturing rates fell sharply, with the larger drop in nonmanufacturing. Thereafter these growth rates diverged greatly: from 1979 to 1986, a period that spans

2. The BLS makes freely available estimates of output per hour by industry groups, which are used here in table 3-1, although it publishes regularly only manufacturing and nonmanufacturing totals.

3. Unlike the output per hour series, multifactor productivity excludes government enterprises. For further description see U.S. Department of Labor, Bureau of Labor Statistics, *Trends in Multifactor Productivity, 1948–81,* Bulletin 2178 (September 1983). See also Edwin Dean and Kent Kunze, "Recent Changes in the Growth of U.S. Multifactor Productivity," *Monthly Labor Review,* vol. 111 (May 1988), pp. 14–22.

TABLE I-1. *Output per Hour in the Business Sector, Manufacturing and Nonmanufacturing, Amounts and Growth Rates, 1948–86*[a]
Output in 1982 dollars

Date	Business sector total	Manufacturing	Non-manufacturing	Manufacturing less nonmanufacturing
		OUTPUT PER HOUR		
1948	7.68	7.19	7.88	−0.69
1953	9.35	8.52	9.74	−1.22
1964	12.80	11.45	13.41	−1.96
1973	15.60	14.35	16.17	−1.82
1979	16.20	15.58	16.45	−0.87
1982	16.31	16.28	16.33	−0.05
1986	17.82	19.80	17.17	2.63
		ANNUAL GROWTH RATE OF OUTPUT PER HOUR (PERCENT)		
1948–73	2.88	2.80	2.92	−0.12
1948–53	4.01	3.45	4.33	−0.88
1953–64	2.90	2.73	2.95	−0.22
1964–73	2.22	2.54	2.10	0.44
1973–79	0.63	1.38	0.29	1.09
1979–86	1.37	3.48	0.61	2.87
1979–82	0.23	1.47	−0.25	1.72
1982–86	2.23	5.02	1.27	3.75
		COMPOSITION OF BUSINESS SECTOR (PERCENT OF TOTAL)		
Total output				
1948	100.0	26.8	73.2	. . .
1953	100.0	29.1	70.9	. . .
1964	100.0	27.8	72.2	. . .
1973	100.0	28.8	71.2	. . .
1979	100.0	27.8	72.2	. . .
1982	100.0	25.9	74.1	. . .
1986	100.0	27.3	72.7	. . .
Total hours				
1948	100.0	28.6	71.4	. . .
1953	100.0	31.9	68.1	. . .
1964	100.0	31.1	68.9	. . .
1973	100.0	31.3	68.7	. . .
1979	100.0	28.9	71.1	. . .
1982	100.0	26.0	74.0	. . .
1986	100.0	24.6	75.4	. . .

SOURCE: Based on Bureau of Labor Statistics data tape and definitions.
a. Includes tenant-occupied housing and government enterprises. Output is gross national product.

the present business cycle up to 1986, the rate was 3.5 percent a year in manufacturing as against 0.6 percent in nonmanufacturing, a difference of 2.9 percentage points. The sector rate was 1.4 percent.[4]

The difference between manufacturing and nonmanufacturing rates increased from 1973-79 to 1979-82, when nonmanufacturing productivity actually fell, and became huge—3.8 percentage points—in 1982–86.[5] In 1982–86 the growth rate in manufacturing was four times that in nonmanufacturing. It was 79 percent above its own 1948–73 rate, whereas the nonmanufacturing rate was 57 percent below its 1948–73 rate. The change in growth rates from 1979–82 to 1982–86 continued a pattern of a greater period-to-period increase or smaller decrease in the manufacturing rate than in the nonmanufacturing rate that was repeated in all the "short" periods shown in the table, starting with the change from 1948–53 to 1953–64. At that time the rate of growth in nonmanufacturing exceeded that in manufacturing.

Output per hour in the business sector as a whole almost stopped growing in 1979–82, and even after a sharp rise to 2.2 percent in 1982–86 the rate remained 23 percent below that of 1948–73. (The rate for the incomplete 1979–86 business cycle as a whole was down 53 percent from the 1948–73 rate.) Because manufacturing output accounted for a little more than one-fourth of business sector output throughout the 1948–86 period (see bottom part of table 1-1), changes in output weights for manufacturing and nonmanufacturing had little effect on the growth rate in the business sector.

The periods shown in the table, aside from 1979–86 and 1982–86,

4. This summary is based on Bureau of Labor Statistics estimates and definitions. The productivity data used are those released before August 1988, when BLS revised and updated its annual series for output per hour. The analysis would not be materially altered by using the bureau's new 1979–87 and 1982–87 growth rates rather than its old 1979–86 and 1982–86 growth rates. In the business sector and nonmanufacturing industries those growth rates differ by 0.1 percentage point or less. The main difference is that the growth rate for manufacturing is lowered by 0.2 percentage point in the longer period and 0.5 percentage point in the shorter period. Estimates for the years before 1985 are unchanged.

5. These growth rates are not adjusted to eliminate cyclical movements. However, my estimates for net output per hour in nonresidential business as a whole showed little difference between growth rates on actual and potential bases in 1979–82, even though the level of the potential series was higher. See Edward F. Denison, *Trends in American Economic Growth, 1929–1982* (Brookings, 1985), table 2-7, col. 13, and table 2-8, col. 10. Most of the differences between the 1979–82 and 1982–86 rates are probably not cyclical in origin.

TABLE I-2. *Annual Growth Rates of Multifactor Productivity in the Private Business Sector and Manufacturing, 1948–86*[a]
Percentage points

Period	Total private business	Manufacturing	Manufacturing less total private business	Total private nonfarm business	Manufacturing less total private nonfarm business
1948–73	2.00	2.03	0.03	1.68	0.35
1948–53	3.14	2.96	−0.18	2.55	0.41
1953–64	2.07	1.94	−0.13	1.79	0.15
1964–73	1.29	1.62	0.33	1.06	0.56
1973–79	0.10	0.52	0.42	−0.08	0.60
1979–86	0.52	2.57	2.05	0.33	2.24
1979–82	−1.49	−0.60	0.89	−1.71	1.11
1982–86	2.06	5.00	2.94	1.89	3.11

SOURCE: Computed from Bureau of Labor Statistics, "Multifactor Productivity Measures, 1986," *News*, USDL 87-436, October 13, 1987, tables 1–3.

a. Includes tenant-occupied housing. Excludes government enterprises. Output is gross national product.

are those used in my studies of economic growth. Their selection was not influenced by comparisons of manufacturing and nonmanufacturing industries. The BLS data for output per hour in "business" differ from my own series for "nonresidential business" in several respects, of which the most important are these: BLS measures output gross instead of net of capital consumption, includes in output the value added in tenant-occupied farm and nonfarm houses, values output at market prices instead of factor cost, and in total hours includes hours paid for but not worked.

The bureau also estimates multifactor productivity, a measure of gross output per unit of labor, capital, and land, with labor input measured by hours paid. These data refer to private business, a category smaller than the one BLS uses for output per hour because it excludes government enterprises. Growth rates for private business and for manufacturing are shown in the first two columns of table I-2. (Nonmanufacturing data are not available separately.) The pattern of change is generally similar to that for output per hour. The growth rate for manufacturing exceeded that for the total business sector by a trivial 0.03 percentage point in 1948–73 but by 0.9 point in 1979–82 (when both manufacturing and sector rates were negative) and 2.9 points in 1982–86. The last figure is even bigger than the corresponding difference

(2.8 points) for output per hour. As with output per hour the growth rate of productivity rose more or fell less in manufacturing than in the whole sector from each short period to the next. The table also compares manufacturing with *nonfarm* private business, a comparison that is more favorable to manufacturing but shows fairly similar changes.

I also have occasion to refer to my own series for *output per unit of input* in nonresidential business. Output is measured by national income, a measure of net national product (NNP). I prefer a net product measure because, insofar as large output is a proper goal of society, it is output net of capital consumption that measures the degree of success in achieving this goal. There is no reason to wish to maximize the quantity of capital goods used up in production. The input series I use as a denominator is broadly similar to the one BLS uses in measuring multifactor productivity but with an important difference. In measuring labor input, I allow for changes in the composition, or "quality," of the persons providing hours worked. These changes refer to the composition of labor by age, sex, and education, and the effect on the efficiency of an hour's work of changes in average hours.[6]

The business sector is often divided between commodity-producing and service industries rather than between manufacturing and nonmanufacturing. The BLS makes available, though it does not publish, estimates of output per hour for these sectors. The pattern of differential change is much the same if the other commodity-producing industries (farms, mining, and contract construction) are grouped with manufacturing.

One common misconception about industry estimates must be disposed of at the outset. Believing that the big difference between recent productivity changes estimated for manufacturing and nonmanufacturing is implausible, some people have reasoned, incorrectly, that the data for manufacturing are the more reliable, that productivity growth in nonmanufacturing industries must therefore be understated because

6. Another difference from multifactor productivity is that structures and equipment receive less weight and other inputs more because my output measure is net of depreciation. Weights in both series are based on the earnings of the various inputs and when, as in the BLS series, output is gross of capital consumption, capital consumption is included in the earnings of structures and equipment.

of faulty measurement of output, and that as a result productivity growth in the business sector as a whole is understated.

This reasoning is quite wrong, as economists familiar with the derivation of the estimates have always understood. Output valued in constant prices in the business sector as a whole is estimated by deflating the final-product components of the sector's gross national product.[7] No use is made of data for industries. The output of the sector is divided among industries later. The total being given, if one dollar too little of an increase in sector output is assigned to nonmanufacturing industries, one dollar too much is assigned to manufacturing industries. Thus estimates of output by industry in no way affect the business sector's total output.[8] With trivial exceptions, the situation is similar for estimates of labor and capital inputs.

In reporting certain criticisms of estimates of GNP by industry (including some made in this study, which were provided before publication), BEA recently published data on the quantitative importance of some of its procedures.[9] I cite this information where appropriate.

One way to examine the recent wide divergence between the growth rates of productivity in manufacturing and those in nonmanufacturing is to seek to explain the different behavior of the two sectors. The other, given more attention in this study, is to examine the reliability of the industry estimates in order to judge how much credence to give

7. To obtain maximum statistical consistency between the input and output series, a slight adjustment is included to conform the current-dollar GNP estimates by final product to the estimates obtained as the sum of national income and other charges against GNP.

8. This is obviously true when the estimates of interindustry sales and purchases are internally consistent or when estimates for nonmanufacturing output are obtained by subtracting manufacturing output from the sector total. The estimates of GNP by industry in constant dollars appearing in the national income and product accounts are, to be sure, calculated independently and are not internally consistent, because the implied estimates for interindustry sales in constant prices differ from identically defined interindustry purchases. But the inconsistency results in the inclusion of a "residual" line, so the industry data still do not affect estimates of the output of the whole economy or its sectors. See *Survey of Current Business*, vol. 67 (July 1987), table 6.2.

9. Frank de Leeuw, "Gross Product by Industry: Comments on Recent Criticisms," *Survey of Current Business*, vol. 68 (July 1988), pp. 132–33. Besides making use of my study, BEA apparently took into account Lawrence Mishel, *Manufacturing Numbers: How Inaccurate Statistics Conceal U.S. Industrial Decline* (Washington, D.C.: Economic Policy Institute, 1988).

to reported divergences in growth rates of productivity between industries.

Measuring Production of Computers

In the BEA and BLS output measures, the movement of the value of computers produced, measured in constant prices, is based on the memory capacity and speed of computer processors and disk drives; the speed, versatility, and resolution of printers; the screen capacity, resolution, number of colors, and number of programmable function keys of terminals; and certain other characteristics. Because of improvements in the design of computers and their components, the power of computers has increased tremendously without a corresponding increase in the labor and capital required to produce computers. For this reason and also because techniques of producing computers of constant power advanced unusually fast, productivity in the production of computer power has grown enormously, and the price of computers per unit of power has therefore dropped enormously according to BEA and BLS.

All the productivity increase in computer production is classified in the nonelectrical machinery industry within durable goods manufacturing. Fully 39 percent of the large difference between manufacturing and nonmanufacturing growth rates of output per hour from 1982 to 1986, and 36 percent even over the longer 1979–86 period, results from the excess of the increase in output per unit of input in computer production over that in production of other producers' durable goods. This exceptional productivity increase in computer production is a very special development that is specific to a single industry and has no general significance in a characterization of productivity changes in manufacturing and nonmanufacturing.

It is also apparent that, by appropriate criteria, the growth of gross and net product has been overstated in recent years because the weights used to compile these aggregates give a greatly exaggerated effect to improvement in the quality of computers. Different kinds of output or capital are combined by use of fixed 1982 price weights. Fixed weights work well only so long as big changes in relative prices that are associated with big changes in relative quantities do not occur. That was not the case with computers. By 1986 the very fast growth occurring in the production of computers, as measured, was receiving perhaps 2½ times as much weight in the growth of business product as it would have received with current 1986 weights. The corresponding sharp drop in the relative price of computers, as measured, meant that a firm investing $40 in computers in the expectation of raising its annual net product by $4 is treated in the constant-price series as if the investment would raise its annual net product by $10. (Before 1982, in contrast, the rapid increase in computer output is underweighted by reference to then-current prices.)

In gross national product, used by BLS to measure output, the additional product made possible by improvement in computers is, in addition, counted twice: in computer manufacturing when computers are made, and in computer-using industries when computers are used. The additional output is counted only once in net national product (in computer manufacturing when computers are made) because the adjustment for computer quality, if accurate, ensures that in computer-using industries a rapid rise in depreciation on computers prevents improvement of computers from ever raising productivity. Both the industry allocation and the timing of the net product increase are, however, contrary to usual practice and the customary interpretation of productivity estimates.

The BEA measure of the constant-dollar value of computers is itself seriously flawed in terms of its objective, because it takes no account of the amounts of direct and indirect labor or other inputs that are required for the use of different computer models, as would be necessary to obtain a series that equated computers of different models by their marginal products. If the gross output of a new model is twice that of an old model, the new computer is counted as twice as much product whether, directly and indirectly, its use requires ten times as much labor or other inputs as the old or one-tenth as much.

The exceptional improvement in the quality of computers is such a special development and has such a large effect on the estimates that it is desirable to treat it as a special case and analyze remaining differences in industry productivity change separately. That is made still more desirable because the impact on output of producing better computers is greatly exaggerated by use of fixed weights and use of gross product to measure production. If current-price weights were used and, in addition, national product were measured after deduction of capital consumption, by 1986 the unusually rapid productivity increase in computer production would have raised the growth rate of output per hour only a little more than one-fourth as much as it does with present procedures. In addition (as the preceding paragraph noted), the way improvement in quality is measured is itself questionable even in terms of its own objectives.

Up to this point, it has been assumed that an allowance for improvement in quality stemming from improved design would be desirable for computers if it could be made accurately. In measuring capital input, however, there is a fundamental conceptual objection to this allowance; namely, that it treats an output gain stemming from an accretion to knowledge as if it were the result of additional saving and investment. Advances in knowledge of how to produce at low cost have been the biggest source of increase in output per unit of input. Determinants of advances in knowledge differ from determinants of saving and investment, so the effect of the misclassification is to make growth analysis chaotic. I conclude in chapter 2 that conceptual considerations make it desirable to eliminate the computer adjustment when measuring not only capital input but also national product.

In chapters 3 and 4 I remove the unusual productivity increase in computer production from the output measure in order to analyze changes in productivity that occurred for other reasons. Sector and industry growth rates of output per hour are recomputed. The effect on output per hour of using improved computers in production is not removed, of course.

Productivity by Industry

The Bureau of Labor Statistics provides estimates of output per hour for two groups of manufacturing industries and eleven groups of nonmanufacturing industries that together constitute its business sector.[10]

10. The BLS also publishes series for detailed industries that, though numerous, cover

After the adjustment to eliminate unusual productivity improvement in computer production is made, these estimates show that in manufacturing the annual growth rate of productivity as measured by output per hour fell from 2.9 percent in 1948–73 to 1.4 percent in 1973–79, and then rose to 2.5 percent in 1979–86. The rate in nonmanufacturing, which was 2.9 percent in 1948–73 (the same as in manufacturing), fell even more than the manufacturing rate to 0.3 percent in 1973–79, and recovered only slightly to 0.6 percent in 1979–86. Within the latter incomplete business cycle period, the rates for manufacturing were 1.0 percent in 1979–82 and 3.5 percent in 1982–86. In nonmanufacturing they were −0.3 percent in 1979–82 and 1.3 percent in 1982–86, still far below the 1948–73 rate. Since nonmanufacturing is almost three times as big as manufacturing, rates for the business sector as a whole—0.1 percent in 1979–82 and 1.8 percent in 1982–86—remained far below the 1948–73 rate of 2.9 percent.

From the 1948–73 period to 1973–79 or 1979–82, BLS estimates show that productivity growth fell in almost all the thirteen industry groups that the bureau distinguishes. After 1973–79, however, changes were extraordinarily mixed.

Within manufacturing, the growth rate of productivity fell by almost equal amounts in durable and nondurable goods manufacturing from 1948–73 to 1973–79: from 2.4 to 1.0 percent in durables and from 3.4 to 1.9 percent in nondurables. Thereafter, the rate for durables fell again to −0.1 percent in 1979–82 before leaping to 5.2 percent in 1982–86. The rate for nondurables, in sharp contrast, partially recovered to 2.6 percent in 1979–82 before dropping to a new low of 1.1 percent in 1982–86. Changes in nonmanufacturing industries also became much more varied.

The disparate movements of productivity in durable and nondurable goods manufacturing after 1979 are strange. No doubt some part of the decline in the durable goods manufacturing rate from 1973–79 to 1979–82 and the subsequent rise in 1982–86 is cyclical in nature. Foreign competition also helped raise productivity in 1982–86 by dis-

only a fraction of the business sector, and that are not related to the aggregates. It has also prepared estimates for two-digit manufacturing industries covering part of the period analyzed here.

placing high-cost production, notably in the steel industry, and also by putting pressure on domestic firms to improve their efficiency in order to survive. But these influences could hardly have accounted for very much of the dip and spurt in productivity estimated to have occurred in durables after 1979. Moreover, cyclical changes and foreign competition also operated, though more weakly, in nondurable goods manufacturing, diminishing their effect on differences in productivity changes between the two parts of manufacturing. The business cycle and foreign competition are insufficient to explain the divergent movement of durables and nondurables.

Chapter 3 describes the ways in which BEA estimates the changes in the output of the various industries. Broadly, it uses three methods. Double deflation—in which the constant-dollar value of the nonfactor inputs that one industry obtains from other industries is subtracted from the constant-dollar value of the industry's gross output to obtain GNP originating in an industry—is used for industries representing 96 percent of the manufacturing total in 1982 but only 21 percent of the nonmanufacturing total, including tenant-occupied housing. Single deflation—in which the constant-dollar value of GNP originating is assumed to move like the constant-dollar value of the industry's gross output—is used for industries representing only 4 percent of the manufacturing total but 63 percent of the nonmanufacturing total. The assumption that labor productivity did not change, or a nearly equivalent assumption, is made for industries representing 16 percent of the nonmanufacturing total. This assumption is not used at all in manufacturing. Double deflation is the only theoretically correct method, but its use may encounter severe statistical problems unless data are highly accurate. In practice, these problems are serious even in industries where the method is used, and data deficiencies are too great to allow its use at all in industries for which BEA uses single deflation or the assumption of constant productivity.

My evaluation of the BEA estimates leads to two main conclusions. First, several aspects of the methodology tend to assign too much of the productivity increase to manufacturing (and commodity-producing) industries and too little to nonmanufacturing (and service-producing) industries, and the size of this bias has increased over time. Second, and more important, the information underlying the estimates is insufficient to convey confidence that growth rates of GNP per hour portray differences among industries accurately.

Apart from data deficiencies, doubts about the value of productivity data by industry arise from their conceptual ambiguity, which restricts their supposed usefulness in interpreting change in productivity. Above all, one must clearly understand that industry estimates, even if they were for output per unit of input, could not identify the industries responsible in any causal sense for increases in economy-wide productivity; that would be true even if value and price data were accurate and double deflation were used for all industries.

This is so even if causality is interpreted in the most direct and immediate sense. No productivity increase appears in an industry when it improves its product without a corresponding increase in its inputs. If the product consists of raw materials, supplies, containers, business services, structures, or equipment, the productivity increase, as a general rule, appears not in the industry making the product improvement but in the industry to which it sells. In contrast, process innovations and managerial improvements in production practices raise an industry's own productivity.

When one attaches a more basic meaning to causality, other problems appear. Many advances in knowledge that raise productivity originate in neither the producing nor the using industry but in some third industry from which technology is transferred, or in an inventor's garage, a government or college office or laboratory, someone's home, or another country. Other changes that raise the business sector's productivity do not raise productivity in any industry. Parts of the gains from improved allocation of resources and increased specialization are in this category.

Productivity by End Product

In chapter 4 I urge that estimates of productivity by industry be supplemented with estimates of productivity for national product classified by end (final) product. That is a very different way of dividing output. In 1982, for example, commodity-producing industries contributed 41 percent of nonresidential business GNP and service industries 59 percent, whereas 67 percent of the final product of nonresidential business consisted of goods and structures and only 33 percent consisted of services. Nearly half the output of service industries consists of inputs into the production of goods and structures.

The conceptual and statistical foundations for a classification of productivity change by end product are at least equal and probably superior to those for a classification by industry. Formally, the two types of estimate encounter a similar but different main problem. It arises because the basic estimates of factor inputs are prepared and classified by industry, whereas the basic estimates of real (constant-price) output are prepared and classified by type of final product. To prepare estimates of productivity by industry, estimates of output by final product must somehow be converted to estimates by industry. To prepare estimates of productivity by final product, estimates of input by industry must somehow be converted to estimates by final product. A methodology to derive input by end product from data for input by industry is outlined in chapter 4. For base years it relies on the use of input-output data and one main assumption; namely, that within a detailed industry, input per dollar of value added is the same for output going to each other industry and to final users. Preparation of such series will be a substantial project but a feasible one.

It is also possible to estimate differences among the growth rates of output per unit of input in the production of different types of final products by relying on changes in their relative prices. Because this procedure requires introducing assumptions likely to be fulfilled only over fairly long time periods having terminal years that are reasonably comparable with respect to cyclical position and price lags, the results are by no means as satisfactory as direct estimates. Nevertheless, in the absence of direct estimates, indirect estimates of differences in productivity change based on price movements are provided in chapter 4 for broad groups of final products.

The study concludes by repeating the caution that deficiencies in the estimates by industry do not imply weaknesses in productivity estimates for the business sector as a whole. I regard annual series for that sector as reasonably satisfactory, apart from the handling of computers.

chapter two

The New Way of Measuring Production of Computers

Rapid productivity change in the production of computers accounts for much of the recent acceleration in the growth of output per hour and output per unit of input in manufacturing. This increase is quite apart from any changes in productivity in industries using computers that may be attributable to computers, a subject I address only incidentally.

The output data used by the Bureau of Labor Statistics in measuring productivity in the business sector, including output of computers, are obtained from the Bureau of Economic Analysis. In its most recent benchmark revision of the national income and product accounts, BEA introduced a new way of measuring computer output. Beginning with data for 1969, when computer output was becoming significant, BEA bases the movement of the constant-dollar value of computers produced on the memory capacity and speed of computer processors and disk drives; on the speed, versatility, and resolution of printers; on the screen capacity, resolution, number of colors, and number of programmable function keys of terminals; and on certain other characteristics.[1] Because of improvements in the design of computers and their components, the power of computers has increased enormously without a corresponding increase in the labor and capital required to produce computers. As a result, productivity in the production of computers, as now measured, has also increased enormously.

The seven sections of this chapter deal with the following topics. In

1. See Rosanne Cole and others, "Quality-Adjusted Price Indexes for Computer Processors and Selected Peripheral Equipment," *Survey of Current Business*, vol. 66 (January 1986), pp. 41–50; and David W. Cartright, "Improved Deflation of Purchases of Computers," *Survey of Current Business*, vol. 66 (March 1986), pp. 7–10.

the first three sections I do not question the use of the new method of measuring computer output and input; in later sections I do.

1. How much have the very special developments in computer design and production contributed to the growth rate of the gross output series (GNP) used by BLS for the business sector? How much have they contributed to the growth rates of gross output per hour in the business sector as a whole, in manufacturing, and in nonmanufacturing? The amounts, which exclude any effects on computer-using industries, are big in manufacturing, appreciable in the business sector, and nil in nonmanufacturing. Some 39 percent of the difference between manufacturing and nonmanufacturing growth rates in 1982–86 is due to the exceptionally large productivity increase in computer production.

2. How much has the exceptional productivity increase in computer production contributed to the growth rates of net national product and NNP per hour in the business sector, in manufacturing, and in nonmanufacturing? In 1982–86 the effect on the business sector growth rate was one-third smaller than the effect on the growth of gross output, but the effect on the gap between the manufacturing and nonmanufacturing rates was, nevertheless, fully as large.

3. How does inappropriate weighting of computers in the series for output bias the series for output per hour and multifactor productivity? How can the bias be removed?

4. How does measurement (by both BEA and BLS) of the computer component of the capital stock by the same new method used for the computer component of gross output affect the growth rates of gross and net output per unit of input, and of multifactor productivity, in the business sector? How does it impair the classification of the sources of growth? In this section I argue that it is not appropriate to measure computer input in the new way and that, if the new procedure is followed, series for total input and output per unit of input, or for the contributions made to growth of output by increases in capital and advances in knowledge, have little use because the classification of growth sources is destroyed.

5. The special treatment of computers changes in an undesirable way the timing and industry distribution of changes in net and gross

output per unit of input. The GNP measure is made to count the contribution of quality improvement in business computers twice. These relationships are explained in this section, which is important for understanding the new BLS industry data.

6. It was shown in the fourth section that, with the new method of handling quality change in computers, the introduction of improved computers should not raise *net* output per *unit of input* except in computer production itself. This section points out that this fact does not explain the productivity slowdown outside computer production, because the slowdown is also observed in *gross* output per unit of input and gross output per hour, which (outside of computer production) are not affected by the way quality change in computers is handled.

7. This section returns to output measurement and questions the use of the new computer procedure in measuring output as well as input.

I conclude by explaining why in the rest of the study I use the alternative series, developed in the first section, that does not follow the new procedure for computer output.

Effect on the Growth of GNP and GNP per Hour

Improvements in design have increased the power of computers enormously without a corresponding increase in the labor and capital required to produce them. Partly for this reason, the new measures of output based on their power imply that output per unit of input has risen far more in producing computers than in producing other products. As a result, the implied price of computers has fallen drastically relative to other prices. The following table gives BEA's implicit deflators for selected years (1982 = 100).[2]

2. Computers are separately identified and deflated in the following components of GNP: producers' durable equipment, government purchases (both federal and state and local), personal consumption expenditures, exports, and imports (a deduction). Before 1983 personal consumption expenditures for computers are included in producers' durable equipment. Deflators for computers in other GNP components are the same as those shown for computers in producers' durables, although types of computers are weighted differently in government purchases. In computations for table 2-1, all components of computer purchases are combined.

Year	Business GNP (BLS scope)	Nonresidential producers' durable equipment		
		Total	Computers	Other
1948	25.7	22.5	. . .	22.5
1972	46.6	46.8	408.3	45.0
1973	49.6	47.3	369.4	45.8
1979	79.0	78.6	146.2	76.8
1982	100.0	100.0	100.0	100.0
1985	109.7	95.2	56.1	105.6
1986	112.0	95.5	44.2	110.5

To appraise the effect of exceptional improvement in productivity in the production of computers, I calculate the amount by which output of computers would have changed, given the amounts of inputs used in their production, if output per unit of factor input had increased only at the same rate in the production of computers as in the production of other nonresidential producers' durable equipment. This calculation can be made without direct data for output per unit of input in producing computers and other producers' durables because the price series just described can be used instead.[3] To do so requires one additional assumption; namely, that the price (including profit) of a composite unit of factor input used in producing computers changed by the same percentage as the price of a composite unit of factor input used in producing other nonresidential producers' durable goods.[4] The error in this assumption is surely small compared with the differences between changes in prices of computers and those of other producers' durables shown in the informal table above. These differences in price movements result from the fact that output per unit of input advanced at a faster rate in computer production than it did in producing other producers' durables.

3. See Edward F. Denison, *The Sources of Economic Growth in the United States and the Alternatives Before Us* (New York: Committee for Economic Development, 1961), chap. 19, and chap. 4 of this study for discussions of the use of prices to infer productivity change.

4. Substitution of the price of noncomputer business GNP for that of noncomputer nonresidential producers' durable equipment would not change the calculation much, as can be deduced from the informal table above.

Table 2-1 compares growth rates of output per hour when the change in output includes the allowance for exceptional productivity advance in computers with growth rates when this allowance is excluded. Differences (in percentage points) between the two sets of growth rates are the same for total output as for output per hour, because the differences stem only from alternative measures of output. Insofar as the output measure is concerned, the differences are also applicable to multifactor productivity. However, that series is also affected by the way capital input in the form of computers is measured.

The allowance for exceptional productivity improvement in computer production is large in recent years. Its exclusion cuts the gap between manufacturing and nonmanufacturing growth rates of output per hour between 1982 and 1986 from 3.75 percentage points to 2.27 percentage points, indicating that 1.48 percentage points, or 39 percent, of the superiority of the manufacturing rate is attributable to this improvement. Even over the whole 1979–86 period some 36 percent of the difference is attributable to it.[5]

Exclusion of the exceptional productivity improvement in computer production has an almost trivial effect before 1979. It reduces the difference between manufacturing and nonmanufacturing growth rates by only 0.02 percentage point, or 3 percent, in 1973–79, and the change is actually in the opposite direction in 1948–73.[6] Hence the exceptional productivity advance in computer production contributes strongly to the improvement in the manufacturing growth rate both absolutely and in comparison with the nonmanufacturing rate. The reason is that the weight of computers in constant-dollar output has increased greatly, mainly as a reflection of the differential price movement. If computer design continues to improve at the same rate, it will contribute to faster growth in manufacturing by an amount that will keep rising as the weight of computers continues to increase.[7]

5. Recent revisions in the BLS productivity estimates, as noted earlier, reduce the gap between manufacturing and nonmanufacturing growth rates over these periods. The allowance for exceptional quality improvement in computers equals 46 percent of the reduced gap in 1982–86 and 39 percent in 1979–86.

6. The negative differential results from the fact that in 1973 computers were significant but in 1948 they were present in only trivial amounts and not given separate treatment.

7. The fast growth and falling price of computers, with the new measure, make the weight of computers and hence the growth rate of real GNP extraordinarily sensitive to the

TABLE 2-1. *Effect of Exceptional Improvement in Output per Unit of Input in Computer Production on Growth Rates of Output per Hour in the Business Sector, Manufacturing and Nonmanufacturing, 1948–86*[a]

Annual growth rates in percentage points

	With extraordinary computer productivity improvement				Without extraordinary computer productivity improvement[b]				Effect of extraordinary computer productivity improvement		
Period	Business sector	Manufacturing	Nonmanufacturing	Manufacturing less nonmanufacturing	Business sector	Manufacturing	Nonmanufacturing	Manufacturing less nonmanufacturing	Business sector	Manufacturing	Nonmanufacturing
1948–73	2.88	2.80	2.92	−0.12	2.89	2.86	2.92	−0.06	−0.01	−0.06	0.00
1973–79	0.63	1.38	0.29	1.09	0.62	1.36	0.29	1.07	0.01	0.02	0.00
1979–86	1.37	3.48	0.61	2.87	1.10	2.46	0.61	1.85	0.27	1.02	0.00
1979–82	0.23	1.47	−0.25	1.72	0.11	1.04	−0.25	1.29	0.12	0.43	0.00
1982–86	2.23	5.02	1.27	3.75	1.84	3.54	1.27	2.27	0.39	1.48	0.00

SOURCE: Data with extraordinary computer productivity improvement from U.S. Bureau of Economic Analysis. See text for the derivation of data without extraordinary productivity improvement.

a. This table refers to the effect of exceptional quality improvement on productivity in computer production, not to the effect of improved computers upon productivity where computers are used. Output refers to gross national product valued in 1982 market prices. The business sector, as in table 1-1, corresponds to the BLS definition.

b. These data are not the same as the data used before BEA's last benchmark revision. The data here imply that prices of computers would have moved like those of other producers' durables in the absence of greater quality change, while the assumption underlying the former BEA series was that prices did not change at all. Note also that a change in base years greatly reduced the weight of computers.

Effect on the Growth of NNP and NNP per Hour

The preceding calculations, it will be recalled, are based on the use of gross national product to measure output. But it is net national product, not gross, that is the object of production and that I and many others believe to be more appropriate for analysis of growth of output and productivity. The effect of exceptional productivity advance in computer production on measured computer output and hence on the growth of NNP per hour differs from its effect on growth of GNP per hour in two respects.

First, this development has raised the growth rate of the net national product of nonresidential business only two-thirds as much as that of gross national product. This estimate is derived as follows. In recent years net capital formation in the form of "office, computing, and accounting machinery," which consists mainly of computers, has been only 49 percent of gross capital formation in that form. Seventy-eight percent of computer purchases (net of imports) has consisted of nonresidential producers' durable equipment, and 22 percent has consisted of consumer and government purchases and net exports. GNP has equaled 112 percent of NNP. The approximate effect on the growth rate of NNP in the business sector as a whole has therefore been $[(0.78 \times 0.49) + 0.22] \times 1.12$, or 67 percent of the effect on the growth rate of GNP.

Second, even though exceptional productivity increase in computer production has raised growth of business NNP less than growth of business GNP, it has enlarged the *difference* between manufacturing and nonmanufacturing growth rates fully as much on an NNP as on a GNP basis. The positive effect of accelerating gross output expansion on the increase in GNP and its equally large effect on the increase in NNP are assigned entirely to manufacturing, but the partly offsetting negative effect of faster growth of capital consumption, which affects

choice of base year for deflation. Each time the base year is moved forward in time, the growth rate of GNP and especially manufacturing GNP during the several years preceding the revision will be sharply reduced provided that rapid productivity improvement in computer production continues.

only net output, is dispersed among all computer-using industries. Faster growth of capital consumption reduces manufacturing and nonmanufacturing growth rates about equally—because manufacturing's 25 percent share of computer depreciation is about the same as its share of nonresidential business GNP—and leaves the gap between the growth rates of manufacturing and nonmanufacturing output that exceptional growth of computer productivity creates about the same for net product as for gross product (which was 1.48 percentage points in 1982–86).

The Weight for Computers in Output and Input

When judged by the usual criteria, growth is overstated in recent years because computers are weighted too heavily in the compilation of gross and net product. Different products are combined by use of fixed 1982 price weights. Fixed weights work well only so long as there are no big changes in relative prices that are associated with big changes in relative quantities, such as occurred in computers. By 1986 the very fast growing computer component was receiving perhaps 2½ times as much weight in real gross or net national product as it would have received if 1986 weights had been used.

The sharp drop from 1982 to 1986 in the relative price of computers, as measured, meant that a firm investing $40 in computers in the expectation that this would raise its annual net product by $4 was weighted in the constant-price product series as if the investment would raise its annual net product by $10. Similarly, for consumers who buy computers up to the point that they derive as much satisfaction from the last dollar spent on them as from an equal expenditure on other consumer goods, by 1986 the fixed-weight series weighted computers as if they provided 2½ times as much satisfaction as an equal expenditure on other goods. Viewed from the standpoint of producers, by 1986 a sale of $1.00 in the form of computers was counted in the constant-price series as the equivalent of a sale of $2.50 of other products.

Before 1982, the base year for deflation, the computer was underweighted relative to current prices, and increasingly so as one goes back in time. In 1973 computers received only one-eighth of their current-price weight in the constant-price series.

One effect of using fixed weights together with the new computer price index is to bias upward over time changes in the growth rate of national product and productivity in the business sector, manufacturing, durable goods manufacturing, and nonelectrical machinery, the bias increasing as the scope of the series is narrowed. The only way to reduce or avoid this bias is to change the price weights used to measure real national product very frequently and link series with different base-year weights to form a continuous series, or to adopt some variant of the approach.[8]

The computer has introduced a similar problem of inappropriate weighting into BEA's capital stock estimates. Indeed, the problem is greater there because the computer constitutes a larger share of business capital stock than of business product. If I were to apply my past analytical procedure to the revised capital stock data (I have not), from 1969 to the base year 1982 underweighting of the fast-growing computer component would cause understatement of the growth of the capital stock and hence of the contributions of capital and total factor input. In that period the growth of output per unit of input would be correspondingly overstated. After 1982, when the computer is overweighted, the contribution of capital to growth and the growth rate of total factor input would be increasingly overstated, and that of output per unit of input understated.

The BLS index of capital input, used in calculating total factor input and multifactor productivity, is a Tornqvist index that uses current price weights and thus avoids using an improper weight for computers. Multifactor productivity is, of course, affected by the use of fixed weights for GNP in the same way as output per hour.

8. This method can be used conveniently only to provide supplementary series for GNP, NNP, and their major components. It would be highly inconvenient if tables providing detailed components of national product were not presented as continuous series in the prices of a single base year.

Inappropriateness of the New Computer Series to Measure Capital Input

The preceding section showed that, given the new computer price index, inappropriate weighting of the computer in real GNP is exaggerating the growth of total and, especially, manufacturing productivity. As of 1986 only two-fifths of the effect of the unusual productivity increase in computer production will remain if current weights are used. The section assumed, however—as do BLS productivity series—that BEA's new computer price index is appropriate for the deflation of computers viewed as a component of both the national product and capital input. But I believe this assumption is wrong. In this section I consider capital input. At issue are the classification of the sources of growth, the timing of productivity change, and the industrial allocation of productivity change.

CLASSIFICATION OF GROWTH SOURCES

The main reason for analyzing economic growth is to be able to answer questions of this type: if we alter any determinant of the level of output by *x* amount, how much will output be altered as a result? Historically, we want to know what determinants of output changed and by how much, and the amount that the change in each determinant contributed to growth.

Among several considerations that should govern a classification of growth sources, two, practicality and causality, are particularly pertinent here.[9] In considering them, I emphasize the dividing line between the contribution made to growth by "increases in capital" and by "advances in knowledge as to how to produce at low cost," two of the growth sources identified in my estimates. In the BLS series they fall, respectively, within changes in factor input and changes in multifactor productivity.

The first consideration is that a practical classification must take into

9. Fuller discussions of classification appear in Edward F. Denison, "Classification of Sources of Growth," *Review of Income and Wealth*, vol. 18 (March 1972), pp. 1–25, and *Accounting for United States Economic Growth, 1929–1969* (Brookings, 1974), pp. 104–10.

account the possibilities of estimation. Any comprehensive classification inevitably requires some estimates that in the present state of the art can be provided only with great difficulty and a large margin of error. But some groupings require estimates that are extremely difficult or even inherently impossible to construct and that alternative groupings do not require. This criterion is especially pertinent to capital, as will be shown shortly.

Second, a useful classification should identify cause with effect. The line between the contributions of capital and advances in knowledge, in particular, should be so drawn that the former measures growth resulting from saving and investment (in the current context, the portion invested in nonresidential business) and the latter measures comprehensively growth resulting from advances in knowledge that permit goods and services to be produced with less input. The distinction is basic because different causes govern the behavior of the two determinants, and the actions that would be appropriate to influence them differ fundamentally. The measure of capital input that I and, apart from computers, BEA and BLS use is, properly, so constructed that capital does not capture the contributions of inventions and other advances in knowledge that are manifested in the form of improved capital goods design.[10]

ALTERNATIVE WAYS OF HANDLING CHANGES IN QUALITY

There are, broadly, four ways in which one can conceive of handling changes in the quality of capital goods.[11] Elsewhere I have discussed three of them and explored their implications at length.[12]

10. However, the distinction between capital and advances in knowledge is slightly compromised by another procedure, to which I return later in this chapter.

11. Changes in quality, as used here, do not include alterations in the mix of some class of capital goods. Suppose in a base year a certain model of truck costs twice as much as another model. Suppose in a later year there are more of the expensive trucks and fewer of the cheaper trucks in the capital stock than there were in the base year. Although the average quality of trucks might be said to have improved, this is a type of quality change that is not under discussion. It causes no systematic problems in measurement or disagreement as to how to proceed: the first truck is simply counted as twice as much capital as the second. The quality change "problem" arises when the quality of one or both models of the truck changes, or one model disappears and is replaced by a new model.

12. See Edward F. Denison, "Theoretical Aspects of Quality Change, Capital Consumption, and Net Capital Formation," in Conference on Research in Income and Wealth,

Method One: Capital measured by cost. The first method is both fruitful and practical. The value, in base-period prices, of the stock of durable capital goods (before allowance for capital consumption) measures the amount it would have cost in the base period to produce the *actual* stock of capital goods existing in the given year (*not* its equivalent in ability to contribute to production). Similarly, gross additions to the capital stock and capital consumption are valued in terms of base-year costs for the *particular* types of capital goods added or consumed. For durable capital goods not produced in the base year, one must substitute the amount it would have cost to produce them if they had been known and actually produced. But a similar modification is required in all deflation or index number problems.

This method is statistically feasible within reasonable limits. Computers apart, it is the only one for which estimates exist, because of the nature of the price indexes used for deflation. With producers' durable goods, only those changes in specification involving differences between the production costs of old and new types of capital goods are usually taken into account; in such cases the adjustment is based on the cost differential. When price indexes for commodities that have not changed are used to deflate those that have changed, a common practice (and essentially the method I have used here to construct alternative estimates for the computer), the effect is approximately the same: a change in quality is reflected only to the extent it involves a corresponding difference in the price charged. The result is also the same when assorted variants of these procedures are used, including the so-called hedonic method as used, for example, by the Census Bureau to measure residential construction.[13]

A point of some importance to the discussion of computers, and to which I return, is the following. If new products are added to price

Problems of Capital Formation, Studies in Income and Wealth 19 (Princeton University Press for National Bureau of Economic Research, 1957), pp. 215–61, esp. pp. 217–34 and 255–59.

13. See comments by George Jaszi and Edward F. Denison on Zvi Griliches, "Notes on the Measurement of Price and Quality Changes," in Conference on Research in Income and Wealth, *Models of Economic Determination,* Studies in Income and Wealth 28 (Princeton University Press for National Bureau of Economic Research, 1964), pp. 404–13.

indexes, with or without deleting older products, the timing of the change may be important. Just after new products appear on the market the ratios of their prices to prices of old products, especially to prices of products made obsolescent during their survival period, are likely to exceed corresponding cost ratios and particularly the cost ratios a few years later when initial production problems for new products have been overcome, obsolescent products have vanished from the market, and price ratios for surviving products tend to correspond to cost ratios that will endure. Because prices of new products have rarely entered price indexes used in deflation until after the transitional period, new products tend to be equated with previously existing ones by normal, or continuing, cost.

Computers apart, all estimates of the capital stock, including those of BEA, use this cost method and are defined in a way corresponding to this method. BEA considers the computer estimates too to be of this type.[14] This seems to me incorrect. BEA does not equate different computers by their production cost but, instead, by the performance characteristics I have enumerated. Unlike the Census Bureau's use of the hedonic method for housing, in the methodology for computers essentially new products are introduced by extending the values for performance characteristics far beyond the range attained by products previously available.

Method Two: Capital input proportional to total output. This method, deriving from the assumption of constant capital-output ratios, assumes that the capital stock moves in proportion to output. It is essential to realize that the method does not yield a measure of capital's contribution to output. For use as such a measure, its result is fatally flawed because the method takes no account of other inputs. For example, if output doubles with a new machine, the new machine is said to be twice as much capital as the old, regardless of whether its operation requires one-tenth as much labor, structures, materials, or other inputs as the old machine or ten times as much. Because it does not

14. The BEA's definition was not changed with the introduction of the new computer series. See U.S. Bureau of Economic Analysis, *Fixed Reproducible Tangible Wealth in the United States, 1925–85* (Department of Commerce, 1987), p. IX, note 5.

take account of changes in requirements for other inputs, it is a nonsense method that I have not heard advocated for many years.

The new measures of quantities and prices of computers are based on the computer's capacity to acquire, store, retrieve, process, and display information. They take no account of requirements for other inputs—labor, electricity, structures, paper, programs, and so on—and therefore appear to correspond to method 2 measures.[15] (A slight qualification results from inclusion in the output measure of production technology that affects the size of computers and hence building space required to operate them.)

Method Three: Capital measured by marginal products. This method requires that not only the effect of a new machine on output but also the effect on requirements for other inputs be taken into account. New capital goods are equated with old ones by their marginal products. The input of a type of machine moves like its contribution to output. If the new good has a marginal product twice as large as the old, it represents twice as much capital. The ordinary capital-output ratio is free to move as it will, in contrast to method 2.

Despite the derivation of the new computer estimates by method 2, much of the support outside BEA for these estimates appears to be based on a belief that they correspond to method 3. In order to continue this discussion I shall suppose temporarily that the results do approximate those that method 3 would yield. This is not likely to be the case, and I am not aware of studies to support the supposition.

Though suitable for some purposes if it could be implemented, method 3 violates both of the classification criteria set forth at the beginning of this section. First, practicality. It is impossible to measure capital by this method with information now available or likely to become available. Moreover, if the new capital can do something that no amount of old capital or other resources could do, equivalence cannot be established even with complete information. Second, even if the method were practical, it would not yield interesting estimates of the

15. I ignore here the consideration that even believers in the constant capital-output ratio have usually applied it to the total output and capital of an industry or the whole business sector, not to the output of a particular process and a particular machine used in that process.

sources of growth. It would ascribe output gains made possible by advances in knowledge, not saving and investment, to the increase in capital.

Even if the new measure of quality improvement in computers really approximates the result of applying method 3, one ends up with a set of inconsistent estimates. Additional output stemming from quality improvement in other capital goods is classified as a contribution of advances in knowledge and raises multifactor productivity, whereas quality improvement in computers is classified as a contribution of capital and raises total factor input.

The Bureau of Economic Analysis, however, regards the new estimates as corresponding not to method 3 but to method 1. Superficially the procedure used may indeed be similar to one variant of method 1, but its results are substantively different from those of procedures used for other capital goods and the difference is crucial in analyzing sources of growth.

In my opinion, if the procedure is construed as an attempt to apply method 1, two aspects make it unsuitable for measuring capital input. The first is the introduction of new products (models) into the price index by comparing their prices and characteristics with older ones in the year they appear on the market.[16] Because the prices of new models have not yet fallen to their longer-term cost, and those of older, obsolescent models still on the market tend to drop promptly, the ratio of the value placed on the new product to that placed on the old product is above what the ratio of their costs would be if both were produced in volume after a learning period. The effect is that not only output but also the capital stock rises more than it would rise if the procedure of delayed introduction that is followed for other new products were

16. They are incorporated in the year of their introduction not only into the new computer price index now used in deflation but also into an additional index that was prepared in the computer study by linking price indexes for overlapping computer models to form a chain index. This index might otherwise be considered a possible substitute for the series for other producers' durables that I have used to replace the BEA computer price index, provided that a method 1 procedure is actually what is desired (which I shall question shortly). Use of this index, as it stands, would cut the growth rates of manufacturing GNP and output per hour in manufacturing by a very substantial 0.4 percentage point a year over the 1972–85 period as a whole, according to BEA. Frank de Leeuw, "Gross Product by Industry: Comments on Recent Criticisms," *Survey of Current Business*, vol. 68 (July 1988), pp. 132–33.

adopted. Consequently, what would otherwise be (and I believe should be) counted as the result of an advance in knowledge is counted as a contribution of capital.

To explain the second and more fundamental characteristic that makes the new computer index undesirable in capital input measurement, I must introduce a fourth concept of capital.

Method Four: Capital measured by consumption forgone.[17] Even the usual procedure for measuring capital, by method 1, overstates capital's contribution to growth and understates the contribution of advances in knowledge, as has been explained by T. K. Rymes.[18]

Suppose new knowledge permits more capital goods, unchanged in design, to be produced with no increase in the amounts of labor, capital, or land used in their production. The usual procedure will show the capital stock increasing as the extra capital goods enter the stock and will credit capital (and total input) with the resulting gains in national product. This occurs even though the increases in output per unit of input in producing capital goods result from advances in knowledge, not from saving in the fundamental sense of consumption forgone.[19] (The Cambridge school of economists has long advocated the measurement of capital by the amount of consumption forgone to provide the saving needed to permit capital accumulation.)[20] But in the past the amounts involved in this difference between methods 1 and 4 have

17. This concept is described but left unnumbered and given regrettably short shrift in Denison, "Theoretical Aspects of Quality Change," pp. 26–27. It differed less from the methods followed by BEA in the 1950s, when that article was written, than from the methods of the 1970s (estimated next in the text) because, as my article noted, BEA's estimates for construction then approximated method 4; small fractions of them still do.

18. T. K. Rymes, *On Concepts of Capital and Technological Change* (Cambridge: Cambridge University Press, 1971), "The Measurement of Capital and Total Factor Productivity in the Context of the Cambridge Theory of Capital," *Review of Income and Wealth,* vol. 18 (March 1972), pp. 79–108, and "More on the Measurement of Total Factor Productivity," *Review of Income and Wealth,* vol. 29 (September 1983), pp. 297–316.

19. In any given year, consumption forgone (hence net investment) valued in constant prices equals the quantity of consumer goods that resources devoted to increasing the capital stock would have provided if devoted instead to production of consumer goods by the methods used in the base year.

20. Rymes traces the history of this concept, which he calls the Harrod-Robinson-Read measure, and contrasts it with what he terms the neoclassical or Hicks-Meade-Solow concept (see note 18).

been small compared with the amount probably associated with the new methodology for computers. In an earlier study I estimated that because I had used method 1 instead of method 4, I had credited "nonresidential structures and equipment" and "inventories" each with being the source of an estimated 0.04 percentage point too much of the 1929–48 growth rate of national income and 0.08 point too much of the 1948–69 rate.[21] Apart from the new computer methodology, amounts after 1973 are smaller.

Economists at BEA regard the new computer methodology as formally equivalent to that used for other capital goods (method 1). I do not agree with this interpretation.[22] But, in any case, the implied increase in output of computers per unit of input is so great that it probably causes more misclassification of growth sources than does use of method 1 rather than method 4 for all other capital goods combined. Use of the new computer procedure in growth accounting would make it extremely difficult to interpret the division between contributions made to growth by capital and those made by advances in knowledge.[23]

21. These amounts refer to the whole economy and would be about one-fifth larger in nonresidential business. See Denison, *Accounting for United States Economic Growth, 1929–1969*, p. 134. In that volume I regarded methods 1 and 4 as two acceptable alternatives. I am now inclined to regard the latter as preferable for measuring capital input in growth analysis.

22. Method 1 requires that "the value, in base period prices, of the stock of durable capital goods . . . measures the amount it would have cost in the base period to produce the *actual* stock of capital goods existing in the given year (*not* its equivalent in ability to contribute to production)." Denison, "Theoretical Aspects of Quality Change," p. 222. The computer methodology appears, instead, to be an attempt to equate different models by their ability to contribute to production (marginal product) as required by method 3 but in fact to represent a variant of method 2, which measures the change in capital input by that in total output.

23. In a communication to the author Jack E. Triplett said that the new method for computers is needed to distinguish correctly between movement along a production function and a shift of the function itself. He cited his "Concepts of Quality in Input and Output Price Measures: A Resolution of the User-Value Resource-Cost Debate," in Conference on Research in Income and Wealth, *The U.S. National Income and Product Accounts: Selected Topics*, ed. Murray F. Foss, Studies in Income and Wealth 47 (University of Chicago Press for National Bureau of Economic Research, 1983), pp. 269–311. Triplett's distinction merely moves the discussion to the question of what should be included in the production function and what should be considered a shift in the function (usually represented in empirical work by a time trend). There are almost as many formulations of the production function as there are investigators. Differences depend (among other things) on the determinants of output that are separately identified and the exact definition of each. Some

The procedure already muddies BLS's distinction between multifactor input and multifactor productivity.

Capital input data based on the new computer deflator are not, in my opinion, suitable for analyzing the sources of growth (including calculation of multifactor productivity) and should not be used. In addition, analysts should consider transferring from capital to advances in knowledge the contribution of additional capital that results from rising productivity in capital goods production.[24]

Timing and Industry Distribution of Multifactor Productivity Change

The special treatment of computers used by business changes the timing and industry distribution of changes in multifactor productivity whether output is measured by NNP or, the BLS practice, by GNP. In the case of GNP, it also alters the size of the total change in output.

Suppose that as of year 0 there is an industry that produces 100

---

investigators identify only the total number of hours worked and the stock of fixed capital, so that changes in anything else that affects output (the qualifications of workers, inventories, the size of markets, misallocation of resources, and so on) cause a shift in the production function. Other investigators identify additional determinants and thus narrow the scope of shifts.

In my studies a shift in the production function is represented by a value other than zero in the residual of a sources of growth table. I have sought to come as close as possible to estimating directly the effect on net output of all its determinants except the state of knowledge so that, in effect, a shift in the production function would mean a change in knowledge of how to produce at low cost and nothing else. I have yet to attain this objective—determinants still grouped with knowledge are identified and discussed in my *Trends in American Economic Growth, 1929–1982*, chap. 3—but the last thing I would wish is to divide intentionally the contribution of advances in knowledge between a shift in the function and a movement along it.

24. Estimates of multifactor productivity by detailed industry for Canada that use the "waiting" concept of capital are found in Thomas K. Rymes and Alexandra Cas, *Feasibility of Measuring Multifactor Productivity in Canada* (Cambridge University Press, forthcoming). The authors use output gross of intermediate inputs, instead of gross or net product, to measure output but that does not affect the calculations for capital. A much simpler calculation would suffice at the manufacturing-nonmanufacturing level of detail. The timing of the Rymes-Cas adjustment to the usual capital series is questioned in an unpublished paper by René Durand and Mehrzad Salem, "Alternative Measures of Productivity Growth in a Rectangular Input-Output Framework," Statistics Canada, November 1987.

computers a year and another industry that uses 800 computers and replaces 100 of them each year. At the start of year 1 the first industry switches production to a new and better, but only equally costly, computer. It continues to produce 100 computers a year. The computer-using industry replaces 100 of its old computers with 100 of the new type each year from year 1 through year 8, when all the old-model machines have been replaced. Thereafter, it continues to replace 100 computers a year, but since a second new model is not introduced, the new computers are the same model as those replaced. What happens to net and gross national product under the two methods?

Suppose that the new constant-price series for the output of computers and for the capital stock of computers (from which input of computer capital is derived) fully and accurately capture the quality improvement in computers. The entire increase in NNP per unit of input resulting from the replacement of each computer of an earlier model with a computer of the new model then appears when the computer of the new model is made, and all the increase appears in the computer-making industry (nonelectrical machinery) within manufacturing. These results contrast with those that would be obtained by applying the method used for other capital goods, which equates new and old products by their cost. By that method, the higher net output per unit of input is spread over the service life of each new computer model and the increase appears in the industry using the computer, not the computer-making industry (except for computers used in that industry). These results also apply to GNP, but when GNP is used (as in the BLS estimates) an additional effect occurs (described in the next paragraph).

The calculation of the superiority of the new computer, if it is to be sensible, must be based on its greater ability to contribute to *net* output over its service life, and I have assumed that this principle is followed. But the new computer is given a constant-price value that makes the new gross capital stock series rise more than it would with the usual method (and that is higher after 1982). Consequently, annual depreciation in constant prices, which is based on this value, also rises more (and after 1982 is higher; before 1982 the value is lower). The quality change in the computer is thus counted twice, when the computer is made and when it is used to raise output. This double counting is not a defect of the computer adjustment as such but of the use of gross product in growth analysis. GNP similarly double counts increases in output that result from increases in the capital stock when they are made possible by additional saving and investment.

At the risk of repetition, I shall try to clarify further the effect of departing from the usual concept by taking the case of a single computer. Suppose one computer of a new model was made and sold to a retail grocer at the end of 1982. The cost and price of the new computer was the same as would have been that of the preceding model had there been no new model, the expected service life was the same (eight years), and the grocer's annual depreciation as it is viewed by the method used for noncomputer capital is therefore also the same. The retailer will use the new computer for eight years beginning in 1983, and for the same scale of operation his costs other than computer depreciation will be $1,000 a year less than with the old model, a saving he uses to increase his payroll by $1,000 in order to enlarge the scale of his operation. If computers were measured like other capital goods, NNP and GNP would be the same in 1982 and $1,000 a year higher in 1983–90 than if the computer had not been improved. The 1983–90 increase would appear in retail trade. With the new method, if its results approximate those of method 3, NNP is $8,000 higher in 1982 and no different in 1983–90 than if the computer had not been improved.[25] The additional $8,000 appears in computer production. GNP is higher by $8,000 in 1982 (in computer production) *and* by $1,000 a year from 1983 through 1990 (in retail trade) than if the computer had not been improved.[26]

The undesirability of measuring capital input of computers by the new method is clear from three considerations. First, because its results are wholly different from those obtained by the method used for other capital with respect to the amount, timing, and industry distribution of changes in multifactor productivity, the sector estimates are undefinable. Second, the method transfers to capital the contribution

25. This timing difference is noted in Denison, "Theoretical Aspects of Quality Change," pp. 226–27.

26. Series for the sector and industries will not, of course, exhibit this bumpy time pattern because the new model will be produced for several years and because new models are introduced frequently.

made by one category of advances in knowledge, even though saving and investment do not change while knowledge does. Third, the timing and industry distribution of the improvement in output per unit of input are contrary to common understanding of what the data mean. In the example cited, common usage would regard productivity measured by use of net output per unit of input to be rising gradually as new computers replaced the old model, and the rise to be occurring in retail trade—a description of the results of using the usual method.

Measurement of Computers and the Productivity Slowdown

The small size of productivity advances after 1973 (except very recently in manufacturing) has been a puzzle, made more so by the enormous investment taking place in computers of rapidly increasing capability. Even though performance might have been even worse without the computer, analysts have sought to explain why the computer may not have aided productivity much.[27]

I have shown that, if the new computer concept approximates method 3, it prevents quality change in computers from raising net output per unit of factor input except in the nonelectrical machinery industry, because any output gain elsewhere is matched by an increase in capital input. This circumstance may help to explain the apparent absence of a productivity response to use of the computer when productivity is measured by net output per unit of factor input. But such a response is also absent in *gross* output per unit of factor input, which counts any productivity gain from computers both in nonelectrical machinery *and* in computer-using industries. It is also absent in output per hour, into whose measurement the computer does not enter at all except as output of the nonelectrical machinery industry. Thus the method used to measure computers does not explain slow growth in productivity as measured by BLS.

27. For an excellent discussion, see Martin Neil Baily and Alok K. Chakrabarti, *Innovation and the Productivity Crisis* (Brookings, 1988), chap. 5.

The Computer and the Concept of Output Measurement

If the new method for computers is inappropriate for measuring capital input, is it also inappropriate for measuring computers as a component of output? I believe it is, not only for computers entering the private capital stock but also for those entering personal consumption expenditures, government purchases, and net exports.

The general method of treating quality change and new products is the same for consumer goods as for capital goods. I have often explained the implication of quality change and new products for interpretation of intertemporal comparisons along the following lines:

> When we say on the basis of the official estimates that total real personal consumption expenditures per capita increased by 52 percent from 1960 to 1976, we are comparing actual consumer purchases in 1960 with the sum of (1) products purchased in 1976 that were identical with those bought in 1960, and (2) products purchased in 1976 that were *not* available in 1960 valued in terms of the products that the resources used in their production *could* have provided in 1976 if used to produce products that did exist in 1960. This is only a crude description of the estimates (which rest on a variety of sources that do not follow wholly consistent procedures) but it is approximately correct. Clearly, the estimates do not take into account either the improvements made in a great range of products without a corresponding change in their production costs or the greater range of choice open to today's consumer.
>
> There is no method of measuring output that would satisfactorily take account of unmeasured quality improvements and expanded range of choice.[28]

A method 3 solution that takes into account the complex of pertinent effects on consumer welfare of new or changed products is no more feasible for consumer goods than such a solution is for capital goods, and for the same reasons. Indeed, as Pasinetti suggests, marginal pro-

28. Edward F. Denison, *Accounting for Slower Economic Growth: The United States in the 1970s* (Brookings, 1979), p. 11.

ductivity theory and the concept of production functions were a direct transfer of marginal utility theory from the household sector of the economy to the production sector.[29]

The new method for computers is a deviation from that used for other consumer products as well as for other capital goods. It prevents a general description of the national product estimates.

With respect to the portion of computers entering the capital stock, it would also be inconvenient and, I think, illogical to use a concept for capital formation and capital consumption that differed from the concept used for capital stock.[30]

Conclusion

In recent years exceptional productivity improvement in computers has been responsible for about two-fifths of the superiority of the growth rate of gross output per hour of work in manufacturing over that in nonmanufacturing industries that BLS reports, and for much of the recent recovery of this growth rate in manufacturing. Improvement in computer design is a very special development. It does not imply any pervasive superiority of manufacturing productivity growth even if the new method of treating quality change in computers is accepted. If it is not accepted—and I have argued that it should not be—then the recent difference between the manufacturing and nonmanufacturing growth rates of output per hour should be reduced by two-fifths.

In the rest of this study, I emphasize the estimates that attempt to equate new and old computers by costs at a common date, while recognizing that they are an approximation to this concept. It will not much matter whether the reader regards them as corrected estimates or as estimates in which the effect of improved computer design upon

29. Luigi L. Pasinetti, *Structural Change and Economic Growth: A Theoretical Essay on the Dynamics of the Wealth of Nations* (New York: Cambridge University Press, 1981), pp. 14–15.

30. As I stressed in 1957 in "Theoretical Aspects of Quality Change," this is not to say that there are not purposes for which a different concept, namely method 3, would be useful. Jack E. Triplett defends the use of different measures for different purposes, but does not explain how historical estimates of the capital stock corresponding to method 3 can be obtained. See Triplett, "Concepts of Quality in Input."

output per hour in computer production is removed. Because the estimates of output per hour are gross of depreciation and do not include capital as an input, estimates for industry groups other than durable goods manufacturing are not affected.

I shall continue to make reference to multifactor productivity and output per unit of input, but I have not attempted to recalculate these series to treat computers like other capital goods.

chapter three

Estimates of Productivity by Industry

The Bureau of Labor Statistics calculates output per hour in the business sector, classified by industry group, by dividing real gross national product originating in each industry by total labor hours in the industry. Although it regularly publishes only the data for the business sector, total manufacturing, and total nonmanufacturing, it makes available to users detail at the level shown in table 3-1.[1] Gross national product is estimated by BEA, total hours at work by BLS. First I review these estimates without questioning their accuracy. Then I examine their derivation and reliability.

Growth Rates of Output per Hour by Industry

The top part of table 3-1 shows average annual growth rates of output per hour, by industry group. The first two columns compare 1948–73 and 1973–86 rates. The latter period is then divided between 1973–79 and 1979–86, and 1979–86 is further divided between 1979–82 and 1982–86. The bottom part of the table shows the differences between each industry's growth rate in each period after 1973 and its 1948–73 rate. The data are adjusted to exclude the extraordinary productivity improvement in computer production. (A note provides unadjusted estimates.)

1. In addition, BLS has recently published annual data for output per unit of input, including materials and purchased services, in manufacturing on a two-digit standard industrial classification (SIC) basis. See William Gullickson and Michael J. Harper, "Multifactor Productivity in U.S. Manufacturing, 1949–83," *Monthly Labor Review,* vol. 110 (October 1987), pp. 18–28. As a separate set of data, BLS also publishes gross output per hour for a selection of detailed industries. These series cover only a fraction of the business sector and are not discussed in this study.

TABLE 3-1. *Annual Growth Rates of Output per Hour in the Business Sector, by Industry Group, 1948–86*[a]
Percentage points

Industry group	1948–73	1973–86	1973–79	1979–86	1979–82	1982–86
			GROWTH RATES			
Business sector, total	2.9	0.9	0.6	1.1	0.1	1.8
Manufacturing	2.9	2.0	1.4	2.5	1.0	3.5
Durable goods	2.4	2.0	1.0	3.0	−0.1	5.2
Nondurable goods	3.4	1.8	1.9	1.8	2.6	1.1
Nonmanufacturing	2.9	0.5	0.3	0.6	−0.3	1.3
Farms	4.6	5.7	3.1	7.9	9.9	6.5
Mining	4.0	−2.5	−7.1	1.6	−4.6	6.6
Construction	0.6	−2.1	−2.0	−2.2	−2.4	−2.0
Transportation	2.3	0.1	1.1	−0.6	−4.2	2.1
Communications	5.2	4.1	4.2	4.0	3.8	4.1
Electric, gas, sanitary services	5.9	0.7	0.1	1.3	1.4	1.2
Wholesale trade	3.1	1.4	0.1	2.6	0.3	4.3
Retail trade	2.4	1.3	0.9	1.7	−0.2	3.1
Finance, insurance, real estate	1.4	−0.4	0.3	−0.9	−2.5	0.3
Services[b]	2.2	0.1	0.3	0.0	−1.0	0.7
Government enterprises	−0.1	0.4	0.9	0.0	0.1	−0.1
			CHANGE IN GROWTH RATE FROM 1948–73			
Business sector, total	. . .	−2.0	−2.3	−1.8	−2.8	−1.1
Manufacturing	. . .	−0.9	−1.5	−0.4	−1.9	0.6
Durable goods	. . .	−0.4	−1.4	0.6	−2.5	2.8
Nondurable goods	. . .	−1.6	−1.5	−1.6	−0.8	−2.3
Nonmanufacturing	. . .	−2.4	−2.6	−2.3	−3.2	−1.6
Farms	. . .	1.1	−1.5	3.3	5.3	1.9
Mining	. . .	−6.5	−11.1	−2.4	−8.6	2.6
Construction	. . .	−2.7	−2.6	−2.8	−3.0	−2.6
Transportation	. . .	−2.2	−1.2	−2.9	−6.5	−0.2
Communications	. . .	−1.1	−1.0	−1.2	−1.4	−1.1
Electric, gas, sanitary services	. . .	−5.2	−5.8	−4.6	−4.5	−4.7
Wholesale trade	. . .	−1.7	−3.0	−0.5	−2.8	1.2
Retail trade	. . .	−1.1	−1.5	−0.7	−2.6	0.7
Finance, insurance, real estate	. . .	−1.8	−1.1	−2.3	−3.9	−1.1
Services[b]	. . .	−2.1	−1.9	−2.2	−3.2	−1.5
Government enterprises	. . .	0.5	1.0	0.1	0.2	0.0

SOURCE: BLS computer printouts (except for computer adjustment). Output refers to gross national product valued in 1982 market prices. The business sector corresponds to the BLS definition.

a. Data are adjusted to exclude productivity improvement in computer production. If exceptional productivity improvement in computer production is included, the growth rates, from left to right, are as follows: business sector: 2.9, 1.0, 0.6, 1.4, 0.2, 2.2; manufacturing: 2.8, 2.5, 1.4, 3.5, 1.5, 5.0; durable goods manufacturing: 2.4, 2.9, 1.0, 4.6, 0.6, 7.6. Other lines are unchanged.

b. Includes agricultural services, forestry, and fisheries.

Declines in growth rates of output per hour from 1948–73 to 1973–79 were general, government enterprises being the only exception among the thirteen industry groups. All industry groups except government enterprises and farms also had lower rates in 1979–82 than in 1948–73, eight of them even lower than in 1973–79. The pervasiveness of the productivity slowdown until 1982 is perhaps the main impression conveyed by the table. Indeed, even 1979–86 rates were below 1948–73 rates except in farms, durable goods manufacturing, and government enterprises.

Cyclical changes depressed growth rates in 1979–82 and lifted them in 1982–86. Despite the boost from the business cycle, in the sector as a whole the 1982–86 rate was 38 percent below the 1948–73 rate. The 1982–86 rate was below the 1948–73 rate in seven of thirteen industry groups and the same in an eighth.

That leaves five industry groups, all engaged in either production or distribution of goods, in which the growth rate of output per hour was higher in 1982–86 than in 1948–73. Both wholesale and retail trade were among them. That the gains for trade have trend significance is doubtful because these industries had seen little or no productivity growth in 1979–82; for 1979–86 as a whole growth rates were well below those for 1948–73, in wholesale trade by 16 percent and in retail trade by 29 percent. In mining the rate jumped very sharply from a large negative figure in 1979–82 to a large positive figure in 1982–86, and for 1979–86 as a whole the rate was down by three-fifths from the 1948–73 rate. In farms, on the contrary, both the 1979–82 and 1982–86 rates were above those for 1948–73. The fifth industry group with a high 1982–86 growth rate is durable goods manufacturing.

The 1982–86 growth rate of output per hour in manufacturing as a whole, at 3.5 percent after eliminating extraordinary quality improvement in computers, exceeds rates in all the earlier periods shown in table 3-1, but such rapid growth is not unprecedented for a four-year postwar period. The rate had been 4.8 percent in 1947–51, 4.6 in 1961–65, and 3.7 in 1969–73.

Within manufacturing, the annual growth rate of output per hour for nondurable goods actually fell sharply from 1979–82 to 1982–86, when it dropped below any earlier period identified in table 3-1 and was only one-third of the 1948–73 rate. But the rate for durable goods manufacturing leapt from −0.1 percent in 1979–82 to 5.2 percent in 1982–86. Large short-term fluctuations have appeared in the durable goods series before; presumably they reflect the business cycle or random fluctuations. But even for 1979–86 as a whole the rate for durable goods, 3.0 percent, was above the 2.4 percent 1948–73 rate despite exclusion of the extraordinary productivity improvement in computer production.

If one accepts the numbers for productivity by industry, it is in durable goods manufacturing that one must seek an explanation for the sharp difference between recent manufacturing and nonmanufacturing growth rates. But there is ample reason to question the reliability of estimates of productivity by industry.

Ways of Estimating Output by Industry

The Bureau of Economic Analysis estimates industry GNP in constant prices by a great variety of procedures, but they are of three general types: double deflation, single deflation, and assumption of constant labor productivity.[2] I first describe the three types, then evaluate them.

DOUBLE DEFLATION

The constant-dollar value of the nonfactor inputs that an industry obtains from other industries is subtracted from the constant-dollar value of the industry's gross output.

A more exact description of the procedure used for mining and manufacturing industries (except petroleum and coal products) is as follows. The constant-dollar value of industry shipments plus the constant-dollar value of the change in inventories is measured by deflating a current-dollar series by a weighted price index for a sample

2. The BEA's estimates in current prices, from which the constant-price estimates are derived, are obtained by adding factor charges (national income) to other charges against GNP. Components that are originally reported on a company basis (except for corporate net interest) are placed on an establishment basis in the preparation of GNP in current prices, published in table 6.1 of BEA's annual national income and product accounts. Table 6.2 provides the constant-price data.

of output components. The value in constant dollars of inputs obtained from other industries is estimated similarly and is deducted from the value of output to obtain GNP originating, valued in constant prices.

The procedure is slightly different for construction, railroads, and electric, gas, and sanitary services. Constant-dollar receipts are obtained either by deflating a current-dollar series by a weighted price index for a sample of output commodities or by extrapolating the current-dollar value in the base year by a weighted index of quantities of output for a sample of products. The value in constant dollars of a sample of inputs from other industries is estimated similarly and deducted from the value of output to obtain a preliminary series for constant-dollar GNP originating. The comparable current-dollar series is calculated, and then the implicit price deflator for GNP originating in the industry is obtained by dividing the current-dollar series by the constant-dollar series. The current-dollar GNP series for these industries obtained by subtracting nonfactor inputs from output, as just described, are not the final series; those are obtained by adding factor and nonfactor charges against GNP.[3] Consequently, the final series for constant-dollar GNP originating in each of these industries is obtained by dividing the final series for current-dollar GNP by the implicit deflator calculated in the way described.

SINGLE DEFLATION

The constant-dollar value of an industry's output is obtained in the same way as in double deflation. This output series is then used to extrapolate the base-year current-dollar value of GNP originating in the industry that is obtained by adding factor and nonfactor charges. This procedure assumes that, in constant dollars, the ratio to output of inputs obtained from other industries is the same in all other years as in the base year.

CONSTANT LABOR PRODUCTIVITY

In the absence of appropriate price indexes for industry output, the assumption is made that no change occurs in labor productivity (some-

3. The main reason for differences between the two types of series for current-dollar GNP is the lack of complete data for receipts or inputs, or both.

how defined). To obtain constant-dollar GNP, the current-dollar value of GNP originating in an industry in the base year is extrapolated to other years by total hours worked, employment, full-time equivalent employment, or persons (full-time equivalent employees plus proprietors) engaged in production. All these variants are intended to implement the assumption of no change in real GNP per hour at work, and yield results that differ only moderately (and almost randomly) from those that this assumption would yield.

I also include in the constant-labor-productivity group industries in which the current-dollar value of GNP originating is deflated by an index of wages and salaries (or employee compensation) per hour, per employee, or per full-time equivalent employee, or by earnings per person engaged in production.

Statistical Problems with the Output Estimates by Industry

All the methods of measuring industry output encounter severe problems, which I now examine.

ESTIMATION BY DOUBLE DEFLATION

Among the three methods, only double deflation is theoretically correct. If BEA used it for all industries and all data were consistent, components of constant-price industry gross output that are not final products would equal constant-price gross inputs that are not factor inputs or other charges against GNP. That would leave the sum of constant-price industry gross products equal to the estimate of business sector output obtained as the sum of constant-price final products plus the statistical discrepancy in the national accounts. This would be true regardless of how good or bad the industry estimates might be. If BEA used the method for all industries but the data were inconsistent, the sum of industry estimates would differ from the sum of the final product estimates (including the statistical discrepancy) by an amount equal to the algebraic sum of the inconsistencies between interindustry sales and interindustry purchases of intermediate products.

T. P. Hill has shown that, though double deflation is the only theoretically correct method, it is unreliable unless the data for output and input are both highly accurate—more accurate than he considers them to be in most instances. This problem arises because estimates of GNP originating in an industry are highly sensitive to inconsistencies between input and output series.

Hill summarizes his criteria for the choice of methods as follows:

> In general, the choice of methods should take into account three factors. First, the presumed reliability of the output and input volume indices; if these are believed to be quite accurate then it is obviously appropriate to use double deflation to measure changes in value added at constant prices. If, however, there are doubts about their accuracy, two other factors need to be considered; these are the extent of the divergence between the output and input indices, and the size of the input/output ratio in the base year. If the divergence is not great and if the input/output ratio is low, then the use of the output index alone as a single indicator will almost certainly tend to give more accurate estimates of movements in real value added than double deflation. Conversely, the only circumstance in which the use of double deflation may be justified in the presence of serious errors is when the divergence between the output and input indices is very marked and the input/output ratio is high.[4]

Within nonresidential business, BEA uses double deflation for all manufacturing industries except petroleum and coal products; farming; construction; railroad transportation; and electric, gas, and sanitary services. (BEA also uses it for both tenant-occupied and owner-occupied housing.)[5] Data for current-dollar output and nonfactor inputs are at least relatively good in most of these industries (construction

4. T. P. Hill, *The Measurement of Real Product: A Theoretical and Empirical Analysis of the Growth Rates, for Different Industries and Countries* (Paris: Organization for Economic Cooperation and Development, 1971), p. 112. In my view, Hill is correct in warning against double deflation in the circumstances he describes, but it does not follow that single deflation provides acceptable estimates. Indeed, in manufacturing the ratio of purchases from other industries to gross output has been rising enough to impart a strong upward bias to industry GNP estimates if single deflation were used. See also my discussion later of single deflation.

5. One-line descriptions of the present industry estimates appear in *Survey of Current Business*, vol. 67 (April 1987), p. 27.

being the obvious exception) or else (as in housing) the ratio of GNP originating to gross output is high.

The most general statistical weakness of the method is that manufacturing, railroads, construction, and utilities share with the rest of the economy the difficulty that price data for interindustry sales are usually inadequate.[6] These data are much less satisfactory than those for the final products of the business sector, most of which are covered by series in the consumer price index. The CPI has received much more financial support than the index of producer prices.

One particular characteristic of the deflation procedure imparts an upward bias to the estimates of GNP originating in the double-deflation group, valued in constant prices, during the 1982-86 period. Price indexes used to deflate commodities purchased by these industries include only domestic prices; except for crude petroleum, prices of commodities purchased abroad are not represented. Prices of imports (valued in dollars) systematically rose much less than prices of domestic output during the 1982–86 period as exchange rates for the dollar rose sharply. Consequently, in this period the price indexes used to deflate industry purchases rose too much to be representative of all purchases. The rise in purchases valued in constant prices, therefore, is underestimated and the increase in the constant-dollar value of GNP originating in these industries is overstated.[7] This bias is probably important only in manufacturing. After 1986 the omission of import prices led to understatement of manufacturing growth.

The BEA indicates that the growth rate of manufacturing GNP from 1979 through 1985 would be reduced by half a percentage point or more a year if import prices were taken into account. The 1972–85 rate, however, would be little changed.[8] Hence the 1972–79 rate ap-

6. It should be noted, however, that some of the possible errors in the GNP of individual manufacturing industries that result from inadequate price data are offsetting within manufacturing as a whole.

7. Some overstatement of the rise in manufacturing GNP caused by import prices would remain in 1982–86 even if the price series covered purchases abroad, because while import shares of purchases rose substantially, fixed quantity weights are used to compile the index. To avoid such a bias, it would be necessary (as noted later) to deflate each type of industry purchase from each source (domestic or foreign) separately and add the components to obtain total industry purchases in constant prices.

8. *Survey of Current Business*, vol. 68 (July 1988), p. 132.

parently would be raised by perhaps half a percentage point and the *increase* in the rate from 1972–79 to 1979–85 would apparently be cut by as much as a full percentage point.

After 1977, the year to which the last input-output table used in the estimates pertained, current-dollar data on the commodity composition of inputs for manufacturing are not available. Total inputs are estimated as the difference between output and GNP originating, and the distribution of inputs among commodities is based on the 1977 input-output table. The very fast growth of industries providing services to business, described below, makes it likely that the share of services in interindustry inputs into manufacturing is increasingly understated in current prices. Because service prices rose more than commodity prices, manufacturers' total interindustry purchases valued in constant prices are increasingly understated and manufacturing GNP increasingly overstated.

This understatement of the rise in interindustry inputs into manufacturing valued in constant prices, and consequent overstatement of the increase in real GNP and productivity in manufacturing, almost surely is further accentuated by an upward bias in the price indexes used to deflate purchases from the constant-productivity industries, as explained later in this chapter. The BEA calculates that if prices of purchased services actually rose 1 percent a year less than the indexes BEA used, then growth of manufacturing output (and hence output per hour) during 1972–85 is overstated by about 0.3 percentage point a year.[9]

Another weakness in BEA's double-deflation procedure is its use of fixed weights in constructing the price index used to deflate each industry's nonfactor inputs. That procedure is necessitated by the lack of annual detail on the composition of the current-dollar values of this series. The preferred procedure, followed in compiling both real GNP measured as the sum of final products and industry gross output, would be to deflate each component of an industry's nonfactor input separately and add the resulting series to obtain the industry's total nonfactor input. The difference between the two procedures is the same as that between a fixed-weight price index and an implicit price deflator.

9. Ibid.

TABLE 3-2. *1982 Business Sector GNP Distributed by the Method Used to Estimate GNP in Constant Dollars by Industry*[a]
Percent of GNP originating in industry group

Industry type	All industries	Estimated by: Double deflation	Estimated by: Single deflation	Estimated by: Constant productivity
	BUSINESS INCLUDING TENANT-OCCUPIED HOUSING			
Total	100.0	40.4	47.9	11.7
Manufacturing	100.0	96.2	3.8	0.0
Nonmanufacturing	100.0	20.9	63.3	15.8
Total	100.0	40.4	47.9	11.7
Commodity producing	100.0	83.9	16.1	0.0
Service producing	100.0	11.6	69.0	19.4
	BUSINESS EXCLUDING TENANT-OCCUPIED NONFARM HOUSING			
Total	100.0	38.9	49.1	12.0
Manufacturing	100.0	96.2	3.8	0.0
Nonmanufacturing	100.0	18.2	65.5	16.3
Total	100.0	38.9	49.1	12.0
Commodity producing	100.0	83.9	16.1	0.0
Service producing	100.0	7.9	71.9	20.2

SOURCE: Author's calculations using U.S. Bureau of Economic Analysis, *The National Income and Product Accounts of the United States, 1929–82: Statistical Tables* (Department of Commerce, 1986), table 6.1.
a. BLS definition of business sector.

The possibility that appreciable error is present is suggested by the presence of appreciable differences between fixed-weight price indexes and implicit price deflators for final product components of GNP (other than producers' durable goods and aggregates that include these goods).[10] The error from using fixed-weight price indexes is reduced by the circumstance that within manufacturing the calculations are made for very detailed industries.

The top part of table 3-2 shows that, within the scope of the BLS series for business productivity, industries with 40.4 percent of the

10. For these data see tables 7.1 through 7.17 and 8.1 of the national income and product accounts. The extreme divergence shown for producers' durable equipment (for which the fixed-weight index rose 3 percent from 1969 to 1982 and 5 percent from 1982 to 1986, whereas the implicit price deflator rose 141 percent and fell 4.5 percent during the same two periods) stems from BEA's treatment of computers. It should be disregarded in drawing inferences about possible errors from using fixed weights when the computer adjustment is eliminated, as it is here in table 3-2. U.S. Bureau of Economic Analysis, *The National Income and Product Accounts of the United States, 1929–82: Statistical Tables* (Department of Commerce, 1986), tables 7.1, 7.4; and *Survey of Current Business*, vol. 67 (July 1987), tables 7.1, 7.4.

base-year (1982) value are estimated by double deflation, including 96.2 percent of the value in manufacturing but only 20.9 percent of the value in nonmanufacturing. By a different breakdown, 83.9 percent of the base-year value in commodity-producing industries and 11.6 percent of the value in service-producing industries is so estimated.[11] The bottom part of the table shows similar data for nonresidential business. Exclusion of tenant-occupied nonfarm housing from the total drops the percentage of nonmanufacturing GNP estimated by double deflation to only 18.2 percent, and that of service-producing industries to 7.9 percent.

ESTIMATION BY SINGLE DEFLATION

Single deflation is the most common method of estimate. BEA uses it for fisheries; all mining industries; petroleum and coal products within manufacturing; all transportation industries except railroads; telephone and telegraph; wholesale trade; retail trade; part of insurance carriers; hotels and other lodging places; personal services; auto repair, services, and garages; motion picture theaters and distribution; amusement and recreation services; health services; legal services; and nearly all (the post office and electric power) of the value of federal government enterprises.

Table 3-2 shows that in 1982 BEA used single deflation for industries with 47.9 percent of business sector GNP, based on the sector's scope in BLS data. Percentages were 3.8 in manufacturing and 63.3 in nonmanufacturing or, by the alternative classification, 16.1 in commodity-producing industries and 69.0 in service-producing industries. When tenant-occupied nonfarm housing is excluded, percentages for nonmanufacturing industries and service industries are higher.[12] Esti-

11. The shares of the same industries in current-dollar GNP were formerly much larger. In 1948 they were about 54 percent in the sector as a whole, 97 percent in manufacturing, 33 percent in nonmanufacturing, 90 percent in commodity-producing industries, and 16 percent in service-producing industries. Changes in estimating methods are not taken into account in this comparison. These calculations are based on data from *National Income and Product Accounts of the United States, 1929–82*, table 6.1.

12. For four BEA industries the division of the business component of industry output between "single deflation" and "constant productivity" is approximate. These are agricultural services, forestry, and fisheries; insurance carriers; motion pictures; and federal government enterprises.

mates for few industries within the single-deflation group are reliable. Broadly, there are two problems.

First, there are few industries for which indicators of gross output in constant prices are highly reliable, and for some industries they are quite unsatisfactory. Insurance, real estate, and trucking and warehousing are areas of particular weakness within nonresidential business.

Second, major industries in the group have low ratios of GNP originating to gross output. To understand the importance of this circumstance, suppose that 80 percent of the value of the gross output of an industry in the base year consists of GNP originating in the industry and 20 percent of other inputs. If the estimator assumes that the constant-dollar proportions are the same in the next year but they are actually 81 percent and 19 percent, the error introduced into industry GNP (and hence productivity) is 1.2 percent, but if the proportions for GNP originating and other inputs are reversed, the error is 5 percent.[13] If the division between GNP originating and nonfactor inputs changes from 67:33 to 66:34, the errors are 1.5 percent for the larger component and 3.0 percent for the smaller.

More than 43 percent of the base-year value of GNP in the single-deflation group originates in retail (24.5 percent) and wholesale (18.7 percent) trade alone. The low ratio of GNP to sales in these industries is a major weakness of the procedure.[14] Ratios of GNP to sales, mea-

13. The reason Hill, in "Measurement of Real Product," considers double deflation even less reliable than single deflation in the absence of complete and accurate data is, in effect, that the ratio of input to output may be estimated to change in the wrong direction. If the proportions are estimated to change to 79 percent and 21 percent, the errors become 2.5 percent and 10 percent. Hill believes that input indexes are usually much less reliable than output indexes and that divergences between the indexes are likely to be cumulative rather than random. He points out that the "best" estimate need not be any of the methods described here, which can be visualized as weighted averages of output, nonfactor input, and factor input series. Some different set of weights, determined by the reliability of the three series, is almost always better if reliability is known. Unfortunately, it is rarely known with any certainty.

14. The quality of the gross output series for these industries appears to be much above the average for single-deflation industries. The BEA divides the base-year value of GNP originating in wholesale and retail trade among a number of types of business, using margins as weights, and extrapolates each component by the constant-price sales of that type of business. The components are then added to obtain GNP originating in the industry. Constant-price retail sales are among the more reliable indicators of gross output, and

sured in constant prices, need change only a little within lines of trade to introduce enough error into the industry GNP measure to distort badly the productivity series for trade.

ESTIMATION BY ASSUMPTION

Industries in which productivity is assumed to be constant, the last category, had 11.7 percent of the base-year value of GNP originating in business (BLS definition). In this category in 1982 were 15.8 percent of nonmanufacturing and 19.4 percent of service-producing industries, by value, but no manufacturing or other commodity-producing industries (see table 3-2). Because industries estimated this way have grown rapidly, the percentages have risen greatly in the past, and they continue to do so.[15]

How much does this method of estimation affect manufacturing and nonmanufacturing totals? Suppose output per hour actually grew 3 percent a year in all industries and was so measured except where the constant-productivity assumption was introduced. The calculated rate would then be 3.0 percent for manufacturing and 2.5 percent for nonmanufacturing (2.4 percent for service-producing industries). To be more exact, this would be the result if all industries were measured directly. But adjustments, plus or minus, are sometimes introduced to bring the sum of industry estimates closer to the independently obtained all-industry aggregate, in which only 6 percent of output is deflated by use of the constant-productivity assumption.[16] Concentration of these adjustments in nonmanufacturing industries other than the constant-productivity industries may sometimes tend to narrow the gap between manufacturing and nonmanufacturing growth rates that the constant-productivity assumption introduces. Any such tendency, however, is restricted by the fact that, as explained shortly, understatement

constant-price wholesale sales are better than the output indicators for many other single-deflation industries.

15. In 1948 the same industries accounted for only about 5 percent of the current-dollar value of GNP originating in business, 8 percent in nonmanufacturing, and 11 percent in service-producing industries.

16. Jerome A. Mark, "Problems Encountered in Measuring Single and Multifactor Productivity," *Monthly Labor Review*, vol. 109 (December 1986), pp. 4–5.

of growth in the constant-productivity industries tends to be offset by overstatement in the initial estimates for other industries.

The industries within nonresidential business in which productivity is assumed to be constant are agricultural services and forestry; banking; credit agencies other than banks; security and commodity brokers; insurance carriers (part); holding and other investment companies; miscellaneous business services; miscellaneous repair services; motion picture production; miscellaneous professional services (consisting chiefly of engineering and architectural services); government enterprises except the post office and electric power; and the small segments of educational services and membership organizations that lie within the business sector.

As this list shows, the bulk of the output of the constant-productivity industries is intermediate product that enters into the production of other industries. Productivity growth in commodity-producing industries estimated by double deflation that use the output of constant-productivity industries is overstated—provided that productivity really increased in the constant-productivity industries and (as seems almost always to be the case) that the price indexes obtained for the products of these industries are also used to deflate the same products when they are used as inputs. Thus the constant-productivity assumption not only reduces measured growth of productivity in the nonmanufacturing or service-producing industries, but also raises it in manufacturing or commodity-producing industries. Purchases of services from constant-productivity industries equal 4.5 percent of total nonfactor inputs into manufacturing, and the percentage is much higher when, as is appropriate, intramanufacturing purchases are eliminated from total nonfactor inputs.

VERTICAL DISINTEGRATION

Vertical disintegration (or "contracting out," used in the broadest sense) is another development that has caused productivity growth in commodity-producing industries to be overstated, probably substantially. This development has two aspects: services that are commonly purchased from specialized firms (such as computer, legal, and accounting services) may increase in importance, and activities that were once performed "in house" (such as the work of temporary office employees or messengers) may increasingly be purchased. Both appear to have occurred on a large scale, often for the same service.

When single deflation is used for the industry that contracts out, the value added by the increased or transferred work remains in the industry for which the service is performed, whereas the additional or transferred man-hours appear in the industry in which the work is performed. In the first industry productivity growth is overstated; in the second industry it is understated except that if the constant-productivity assumption is used, *additional* understatement does not occur.

When double deflation is used for the industry that contracts out, the productivity series for that industry would not be impaired if all data were complete and accurate. But that is never the case.

Vertical disintegration by farms, a double-deflation industry, combined with use of the constant-productivity assumption for agricultural services appears to cause great overstatement of the growth of output per hour in farms. Output of "agricultural services, forestry, and fisheries" (classified in services by BLS) consists largely of inputs to farms. The number of persons engaged in production in agricultural services, forestry and fisheries equaled 4 percent of the number on farms in 1948 and exploded to 17 percent in 1973, 27 percent in 1979, and 46 percent in 1986.[17] Because farms is a double-deflation industry, the transfer of work to agricultural services does not in itself artificially raise farm productivity. But all the increase in productivity in producing agricultural services that are used by farms is ascribed to farming. The resulting distortion is big and has greatly increased over time as the agricultural service industry has expanded. The following table compares annual growth rates (in percent) of real GNP per person employed in the industry division "agriculture, forestry, and fisheries," and in its farm component, which even in 1986 still represented over 84 percent of its total constant-dollar value.[18]

17. Unfortunately, agricultural services cannot be examined separately because BEA no longer provides separate data for them. But the private forestry industry is of negligible size, and fisheries employment is neither large nor fast growing. In 1981 agricultural service employment was almost nine-tenths of the total.

18. The table is calculated from *National Income and Product Accounts of the United States, 1929–82*, and *Survey of Current Business*, July 1987, tables 6.2, 6.10B.

Period	Agriculture, forestry and fisheries	Farms	Excess of rate for farms
1948–73	3.5	3.9	0.3
1973–86	3.3	4.8	1.5
1973–79	1.4	2.3	0.9
1979–86	4.9	7.0	2.0
1979–82	5.6	7.3	1.7
1982–86	4.4	6.7	2.3

By 1982–86 the growth rate for farms exceeded that for the industry division by 2.3 percentage points, or more than one-half.[19] This difference was seven times as much as in 1948–73.

Three other industries that have grown greatly and whose combined output is mainly input to other industries are business services, legal services, and miscellaneous professional services (which are dominated by engineering and architectural services). Their combined employment (persons engaged in production) grew from 856,000, or 1.8 percent of total private business employment, in 1948 to 7,646,000, or 9.2 percent of the total, in 1986.[20] Business services alone grew from 382,000 in 1948 to 5,012,000 in 1986, when the industry employed many more people than the two largest two-digit manufacturing industries combined, and over one-fourth as many as all manufacturing. All three are constant-productivity industries, so that the increase in their productivity is ascribed to the industries using their services, including manufacturing and other commodity-producing industries as well as other service-producing industries.

19. The rate implied for agricultural services, forestry, and fisheries, which enters into the total for services, was 0.0 in 1982–86 and had been negative in all earlier periods—by as much as 2.1 percent in 1973–79. This series reflects some combination of mix changes, changes in full-time hours, and estimated changes in output per hour in fisheries. Ibid.

20. In the absence of the exact number of persons engaged in production in private business employment, I use as the denominator in this calculation the number in private industry minus the numbers in educational services, social services and nonprofit membership organizations, and private households. *National Income and Product Accounts of the United States, 1929–82*, and *Survey of Current Business*, July 1987, table 6.10B.

The *increase* in the percentage of business employment that is located in the three industries has itself increased steadily, from 0.14 percentage point a year in 1948–73 to 0.21 point in 1973–79, 0.35 point in 1979–82, and 0.44 point in 1982–86. Consequently, use of the constant-productivity assumption in the three industries has caused productivity growth elsewhere, including manufacturing, not only to be overstated but also to be overstated by increasing amounts.[21] Meanwhile the increasing weight of constant-productivity industries serving manufacturing has been an increasing drag on measured productivity growth in nonmanufacturing. The upward bias the constant-productivity industries exerted on the rate of productivity growth in manufacturing and the downward bias they exerted on the rate in nonmanufacturing help explain the persistent tendency for manufacturing rates to rise more, or fall less, than nonmanufacturing rates throughout the postwar period, a tendency noted in the discussion of table 1-1.

The preceding remarks refer to the ascription to manufacturing and other customer industries of productivity gains really occurring in industries that supply them with services. But vertical disintegration has still another effect. Although productivity data for manufacturing, a double-deflation industry like farming, would not be impaired by the mere shift of work to other industries if the shift were reflected in the estimates of purchased nonfactor inputs, it probably is not fully reflected after 1977, the year to which the last input-output table incorporated in the estimates refers. If it is not, the effect is to overstate productivity growth in manufacturing after 1977 both absolutely and relative to that of earlier years.[22]

ADJUSTMENTS FOR CONSISTENCY

It has already been mentioned that BEA's initial estimates by industry are often adjusted to bring their sum closer to the independently determined all-industry total. The BEA states that such adjustments

21. This is true unless productivity growth in the three service industries was actually falling enough to offset the increasing weight of the industries.

22. Even when all data correctly reflect the transfer of an activity, if GNP per hour in the activity transferred differs from GNP per hour in the industry losing the activity or that receiving it, the transfer will change output per hour in one or both industries affected and complicate interpretation of changes in industry productivity. However, the result will not be incorrect.

raised the 1972–85 growth rate of real manufacturing GNP from 2.0 to 2.7 percent, or by 0.7 percentage point. The 1979–85 rate was raised by only 0.1 percentage point.[23] This implies that the 1972–79 rate was raised by about 1.2 percentage points, which greatly alters comparisons of the 1972–79 rate with rates in other periods.

Such adjustments are entirely proper. When industry estimates of GNP do not agree with the most reliable estimate of their total, they are improved, on the average, by adjusting them so that they do agree. All industries can be adjusted by the same percentage or the adjustment can be concentrated in industries believed most likely to be responsible for the discrepancy. The need to make large adjustments, however, suggests that both the initial and final estimates by industry were unreliable.

Estimates of Hours of Work

Besides problems with output data there are lesser problems with data for hours at work. Most stem from gaps in information, notably the lack of establishment data for hours of salaried employees in manufacturing and for some other groups. Total hours worked by the self-employed, which are based on the Current Population Survey, often behave erratically and in recent years have increased surprisingly. In addition, there are inconsistencies between BEA output data and the BLS employment data that enter into BLS's calculations of man-hours.

Certain to introduce a persistent bias is BEA's underground economy adjustment. To understand the problem, one must recall that the output series used to measure output per hour is obtained as the sum of employee compensation, proprietors' income, other factor income, and nonfactor charges against GNP. (The series is then deflated by use of product prices.) In estimating wages and salaries (as well as employment) after 1950, BEA includes an increasing allowance for undercoverage in data reported by the state unemployment compensation and other statistical reporting systems. The Bureau of Labor Statistics

23. *Survey of Current Business*, July 1988, p. 132.

makes no corresponding allowance in deriving the employment series it uses in obtaining total hours.

The upward adjustment to wages and salaries was equal to 0.20 percent of business wages and salaries in 1952 and to 1.66 percent in 1984. About 95 percent of the adjustment is allocated to nonmanufacturing industries. The apparent overstatement of growth rates of output per hour resulting from the absence of a corresponding adjustment of total hours is as follows (in percentage points):[24]

Period	*Business sector*	*Manufacturing*	*Nonmanufacturing business*
1948–72	0.03	0.00	0.05
1972–84	0.07	0.01	0.09
1972–77	0.13	0.02	0.18
1977–82	0.03	0.01	0.03
1982–84	0.03	0.01	0.03

Contrary to biases in output measurement, this inconsistency causes productivity growth to be overstated in nonmanufacturing relative to manufacturing, but the difference is small except in 1972–77, when it is 0.16 percentage point.[25]

Inconsistent procedures introduce two other types of error, but they are small and may be erratic rather than persistent in direction. First, the Bureau of Economic Analysis uses BLS annual data reported under the unemployment compensation program for covered wages and salaries (which help determine output) for the entire year and employment in all months, whereas the BLS employment series that is used to calculate productivity makes use of employment data from the unemployment compensation program only for March and uses a sample to obtain interpolated estimates for other months. Second, to extrapolate

24. Calculated from "Wages and Salaries" lines in *Survey of Current Business*, vol. 65 (December 1985), p. 5, table 4; *National Income and Product Accounts of the United States, 1929–82*, table 1.15; and *Survey of Current Business*, July 1987, table 1.15.

25. The periods used in this table differ from those used elsewhere because BEA has published data only for certain years.

output in the constant-productivity industries, BEA uses a number of variants of labor input (detailed earlier), whereas in compiling total hours BLS uniformly uses estimates of man-hours. The result of dividing BEA output by BLS man-hours may not be the one intended, constant output per hour, though most deviations are probably small.

Conclusion

The inconsistencies between BEA procedures for calculating output and BLS procedures for hours probably have only a minor effect on differentials in productivity changes between manufacturing and nonmanufacturing. Thus the conclusions I reached on the basis of output data need not be modified.

One conclusion is that industry productivity data may be strongly biased toward the assignment of too much of productivity growth to manufacturing and other commodity-producing industries. A second conclusion is that there are solid reasons to believe this bias has been increasing. These include the combination of a rise in the share of imports in manufacturing inputs in 1982–86, a fall in the prices of imports relative to prices of domestic goods, and the omission from the input price index of the prices of commodities purchased abroad; the rising weight of constant-productivity industries in the nonmanufacturing industry total; the increasing use by manufacturers and farmers of inputs from the constant-productivity industries for which price increases are probably overstated; and since 1977 the probable increase by manufacturers in their use of inputs from service industries as a whole. Unfortunately, I have no way to measure the full size of the biases. A third and even more important conclusion is that industry data are simply unreliable.[26] All these, and especially the last, may

26. I have not enumerated all the problems of estimation in this chapter. There are problems arising from the use of leased property and problems of converting commodity price data to estimates appropriate for deflation of industry sales and purchases. There are also many problems associated with industry classification, such as identifying the industry to which establishments belong and reclassifying them when principal products change, reclassifying property income of multi-industry firms, and maintaining continuity when the standard industrial classification is changed. Moreover, one cannot ensure that imports included in purchases by double-deflation industries are statistically consistent with imports

help to explain the recent divergence between productivity growth in manufacturing and nonmanufacturing.

I do not, of course, claim that there is firm, positive proof that manufacturing productivity growth, excluding unusual productivity improvements in computer production, has *not* suddenly bounded ahead of nonmanufacturing productivity, still less that there are *no* developments that may have helped it to do so.

Closing of the least productive manufacturing plants under pressure of foreign competition provides one special (though not particularly comforting) reason that manufacturing productivity growth may have picked up since 1982. The reported 1982–86 productivity acceleration in manufacturing occurred in durable goods. In some of those industries, particularly steel, increasing import competition and loss of export markets after 1982 led to an abandonment of capacity in the United States. Net merchandise exports of durable goods, valued in 1982 dollars, amounted to −$3.4 billion in 1982, −$69.3 billion in 1984, and −$95.0 billion in 1986.[27] Since it may be assumed that production displaced by import competition was mainly high-cost output, its diversion to foreign countries presumably had a positive effect on average American productivity and contributed to the sharp productivity increase reported for durable goods manufacturing in this period. Moreover, intensified import competition led durable goods producers, particularly automobile manufacturers, to take steps to increase efficiency that probably would not have been undertaken otherwise. The quantitative effect of these developments on productivity is unknown.

as measured in calculating the annual net export component of the GNP series obtained by summing expenditures for final products.

27. *National Income and Product Accounts of the United States, 1929–82*, table 4.2; and *Survey of Current Business*, July 1987, table 4.2.

chapter four

Productivity by End Product: A Proposal

Popular writers and even some professional economists discuss "the services" without drawing a clear distinction between service industries and final products that are services. Yet they are enormously different. The following table divides the GNP originating in the nonresidential business sector in 1982 by type of end (final) product and by industry (amounts in billions of dollars):[1]

	Amount	*Percent*
Nonresidential business GNP	2,404.2	100.0
By end product		
Goods and structures	1,618.5	67.3
Services	785.7	32.7
By industry		
Commodity producing	974.9	40.6
Services	1,429.3	59.4

Some 67.3 percent of the value of the 1982 final product of the nonresidential business sector consists of goods and structures, but only 40.6 percent was created in commodity-producing industries (farms, mining, construction, and manufacturing). Therefore, *at most* 60 percent (40.6/67.3) of the value of goods and structures originated in commodity-producing industries. This percentage is an upper limit that would be applicable if all the value of final products classified as services were created in the service industries. But the value of final

1. Author's calculations using data from the U.S. Bureau of Economic Analysis and the U.S. Bureau of Labor Statistics.

products that are services includes parts of the output of commodity-producing industries. Examples are the fuel used to run the airplanes, trains, and buses that consumers ride and to heat the theaters and operate the amusement parks that they attend; the fabrics used in shops that reupholster their furniture; the grease that lubricates their cars; and the plastic that fills their teeth.

Conversely, of the output of service industries, at most 55 percent (32.7/59.4) ends up as services in the distribution of final products. The true percentage is less, since the value of service end products includes output of commodity-producing industries.

Nearly all efforts to measure productivity change in parts of the business economy have focused on industries. Little attention has been devoted to end products. But the conceptual and statistical foundations for a classification of productivity change by end product are at least equal and probably superior to those for a classification by industry. And there is at least as much reason to wish to classify productivity by end product as by industry.

Formally, the two kinds of estimates face the same problem: how to combine the basic estimates of factor inputs (labor, capital, and land), prepared and classified by industry, with the basic estimates of real (constant-price) output, prepared and classified by type of final product.[2] To prepare estimates of productivity by industry, one must somehow convert estimates of output by final product to estimates by industry. To prepare estimates of productivity by final product, one must somehow convert estimates of input by industry to estimates by final product.

Conceptual Problems with Productivity by Industry

Some of the *statistical* reasons for distrusting the estimates of output by industry were examined in chapter 3. One important and pervasive reason is the paucity of accurate price data for intermediate products; another is that real value added by industry is uncomfortably sensitive

2. Apart from an adjustment to ensure that the *current-dollar* total agrees with that obtained as the sum of income shares and other charges against GNP.

to estimation errors resulting from data gaps and inconsistencies, while the substitution of indexes of gross output or labor input introduces major biases.

Even greater doubts about the value of productivity data by industry arise from their *conceptual* ambiguity, which greatly restricts their supposed usefulness in interpreting productivity change. Above all, one must clearly understand that industry estimates of output per unit of input would not identify the industries responsible in any causal sense for increases in economy-wide productivity even if value and price data were accurate and double deflation were used for all industries.

That is true even if causality is interpreted in the most direct and immediate sense. Consider productivity increases stemming from advances in knowledge. As a general rule, process innovations and managerial improvements in production practices, with no change in the characteristics of an industry's products, do raise output per unit of input, multifactor productivity, and output per hour in the industry introducing the improvement. But no increase appears in an industry's productivity if it improves its product without correspondingly increasing the labor, capital, and land entering into its production. If the product is intermediate, the productivity increase appears instead in the industry that consumes the better product and thereby reduces its costs.[3]

To appreciate the full importance of this fact, one must understand that not only materials, supplies, containers, and business services but also structures and equipment are intermediate products in this context. When a manufacturer of machinery spends money to develop and introduce a better machine, it is not the productivity of his industry but that of the industry using the machine that is enhanced.[4] This circumstance—that productivity increases resulting from improved capital goods and other intermediate products appear in the consuming industry—has complicated the task of investigators who have sought to evaluate the effects of research and development expenditures by cor-

3. As noted in chapter 2, if the product is final, measured productivity does not increase anywhere; therefore, no question of industry allocation arises.

4. In the new BLS estimates the computer is an exception to this generalization; see chapter 2.

relating such expenditures by industry with changes in productivity in the same industry.

When one attaches a less restricted meaning to causality, other problems appear. Many advances in knowledge that raise productivity originate in neither the producing nor the using industry but in some third industry from which technology is transferred. Or they may not originate in any industry within the business sector, but instead in an inventor's garage, a government or college office or laboratory, someone's home, or another country. If one considers the whole process from scientific principle through adaptation of technology to a particular industrial use, it becomes obvious that most improvements have many parents.

Productivity increases in the economy often result from the total or partial replacement of industries by others. Plastics replace metals, photocomposition replaces metal typesetting, or business travelers switch from trains to airplanes. If the productivity gain can be traced at all in such cases, it appears in the industries purchasing from the new industry instead of the old.

One should also recognize that some changes in the productivity of the business sector appear in no industry at all if the data are accurate. Part of the gain from improved allocation of resources among industries is such an instance. In particular, the shift of excess labor out of farming not only raised productivity in farming by reducing underutilization of labor but also raised economy-wide productivity by shifting labor to activities in which the marginal product of fully utilized labor has a higher value. Again, growth in the size of markets raises output per unit of input in the business sector by permitting greater specialization among industries, an adaptation that need not raise output per unit of input in any industry.

The characteristics of industry data I have described make them unsatisfactory if one seeks to go from cause to effect, or even to interpret changes, and I do not see how the defects can be remedied. Whatever principle one might like for the industrial allocation of productivity change, information to implement it uniformly is absent.

Nevertheless, it is not my intention to discourage preparation and analysis of estimates of output and productivity by industry, which sometimes seem useful despite their deficiencies. One cannot help being impressed that the productivity slowdown appeared in almost all major industries in almost all industrial countries after 1973. This is useful information even if it means only that the slowdown was so pervasive that it would appear no matter how one subdivided economic activity.[5] I do, however, urge exploration of alternative estimates in which business gross national product or, better, net national product, is subdivided by end product instead of industry.

Direct Estimates of Productivity by End Product

Estimates of productivity by end product are a natural extension of the present statistical system. Besides asking what happened to productivity in farming, various manufacturing industries, transportation, personal service industries, or retail trade, one would ask what happened to productivity within nonresidential business in providing ultimate consumers (households, nonprofit organizations, governments, and foreigners) with food, clothing, personal services, or munitions. Provision of final products is, after all, the object of an economic system. Changes in the composition of final output constitute an important area of research for economists, marketers, and business generally. By their dominant influence on relative prices, differential changes in productivity strongly affect the composition of output.

Estimates of GNP and NNP by final product are available from the Bureau of Economic Analysis. Their preparation is not free from problems, but it encounters no significant problem that does not also affect

5. The BLS estimates that divide manufacturing output in four countries among thirteen industrial components show a slowdown in fifty-one of fifty-two cases. (Arthur Neef and Edwin Dean, "Comparative Changes in Labor Productivity and Unit Labor Costs by Manufacturing Industry: United States and Western Europe," Bureau of Labor Statistics paper prepared for presentation at the American Enterprise Institute Conference on Interindustry Differences in Productivity Growth, Washington, D.C., October 11–12, 1984.) A slowdown occurred in almost all industrial and Eastern European countries, in most U.S. manufacturing and nonmanufacturing industries, and even in the regions of the United States.

estimates by industry. And the conceptual and statistical problems of allocating changes in real product among industries do not arise.

It is necessary, however, to estimate inputs by end product: man-hours to derive output per man-hour; man-hours, capital, and land to derive multifactor productivity (BLS concept); and characteristics of labor in addition for output per unit of factor input (my concept). Insofar as satisfactory estimates of input are available by industry, they can be converted to estimates by end product by introducing one assumption; namely, that *within each industry* input per dollar of value added is the same for output going to each other industry and to final users. To implement this assumption, *current-price* data for value added are, of course, the appropriate ones. Estimates of value added by industry in constant prices are not needed and could not be used without bringing in the problems present in measuring productivity by industry.

The assumption is best for output per unit of input, where it will hold unless within an industry the earnings of inputs vary in producing different products. But it should not be bad even for output per man-hour, for which the assumption also requires that *within an industry* the quality of labor, and factor proportions, be the same in adding value to different products of the industry. In any such estimation, of course, one expects accuracy in the final results to benefit from the tendency for errors in detail to offset one another.

To implement this assumption requires using the input-output tables prepared by BEA. The key tables allocate the value of final products (counting gross capital formation as final) among the industries contributing value added to this value.[6] A complication is that BEA uses producers' values and does not provide industrial detail for transportation or for wholesale and retail trade in the tables. Nonetheless, the data exist within the input-output system to convert the tables to purchasers' values and thus to obtain necessary detail for trade margins and transportation. To do so is a considerable but by no means prohibitive task.

In these tables BEA delineates industries in such a way as to maxi-

6. These are tables 3 and 5 in the input-output accounts.

mize their homogeneity with respect to products—partly by transferring the production of secondary products to the industry in which they are primary.[7] That is an advantage for the purpose at hand, but it does make it more difficult to match factor inputs with input-output industries. However, BEA has long prepared employment estimates by input-output industries, and beginning with the 1977 input-output table has introduced similar estimates for total hours. Data for inventories and fixed capital, now prepared by BEA on what is essentially a two-digit standard industrial classification (SIC) basis, would need to be adjusted for comparability with input-output industries.

The practicality of using input-output tables to derive estimates of employment by end product category was demonstrated in 1965 by Jack Alterman, then of BLS, who used the 1958 input-output table and the assumption I have stated to obtain a table providing total employment (direct and indirect) per billion dollars of product delivered to final users, by component.[8] Alterman showed employment for eighty-two components of final demand (counting a few synthetic components); he stayed within the input-output framework in that his categories of final demand were deliveries to final demand by input-output industries. The BLS has used similar procedures for later base years in preparing employment projections, but tables like Alterman's have apparently not been assembled.[9]

Complete data for input-output tables are available only every fifth year. Initially, estimates would be prepared for these years. Subsequently, procedures for interpolation and extrapolation would have to be developed so as to provide annual estimates for all years, including

7. Secondary products, however, are assumed to have the input characteristics of the industry from which they are transferred. It is arguable that these characteristics are more like those of the industry to which they are transferred. This assumption has sometimes been made, but it complicates the balancing of an input-output table.

8. Jack Alterman, "Interindustry Employment Requirements," *Monthly Labor Review,* vol. 88 (July 1965), pp. 841–50. The table refers to 1962. Its updating from 1958 used a time series for productivity by industry, which would not be permissible in a study such as I propose. Alterman notes that to use the table to estimate the employment effect of future changes on final demand, one must assume that increased output will require proportionate increases in employment. No such assumption is needed in the use I propose.

9. See U.S. Department of Labor, Bureau of Labor Statistics, *Projections 2000,* Bulletin 2302 (March 1988).

recent ones. The amount and type of detail in which the estimates would be prepared or published can be established only after investigation and experimentation.

Insofar as the end products themselves are concerned, the opportunity for great flexibility in establishing a classification is apparent from the fact that the gross (or net) national product of nonresidential business valued in constant dollars is published in great detail in BEA's annual national income and product accounts (NIPA). They show about 180 product components, including 60 for personal consumption expenditures, 33 for government purchases, 10 for exports, 11 for imports, 28 for private structures, 24 for producers' durables, and 13 for the change in business inventories.[10] Depreciation is available for 14 types of structures and 22 of equipment in BEA's tangible wealth reports.[11] Additional published and unpublished detail is available. I stress the availability of detail not to suggest equal detail in productivity estimates, but to point out the range of choice available in grouping components into a smaller number of categories.

Data for factor inputs and input characteristics, when they exist at all by industry in suitable form, are usually available in considerable industry detail. The BLS provides annual employment and hours estimates on an SIC basis, and BEA not only prepares annual estimates consistent with the national accounts but also estimates for input-output industries in benchmark years. The BEA has annual capital stock data on the essentially two-digit SIC basis used in the national accounts. Data on land are readily available only for farming.[12]

The input-output tables themselves are available in great detail. As already noted, in published data trade is an exception, but margins are available by line of business on the worksheets.

In summary, estimates of output per hour and of multifactor produc-

10. Data are in NIPA tables 2.5, 3.8B, 3.10, 4.2, 4.4, 5.4, 5.5, 5.7, and 5.9. A few of the published personal consumption expenditure components need adjustment to exclude output of nonprofit organizations. The inventory data are by industry; different detail is published elsewhere by BEA.

11. See U.S. Bureau of Economic Analysis, *Fixed Reproducible Tangible Wealth in the United States, 1925–85* (Department of Commerce, June 1987), table A4.

12. However, BEA's future plans for its national wealth estimates include research on land.

tivity, classified by end product, appear at least as feasible to develop as estimates by industry.[13] Their preparation will be a substantial but worthwhile research project. As in all such projects, the details of classification and methodology can be established only as the work proceeds. Estimates of output per unit of input, for which labor input must be adjusted for changes in quality, must await development of satisfactory estimates of labor input by industry.

Indirect Estimates of Productivity by End Product

One can estimate changes in output per unit of input for broad final product components even without measures of input for such components, provided that total output and input (and hence output per unit of input) of the nonresidential business sector as a whole are known. One critical assumption is required: that over the period analyzed the percentage change in the price of a composite unit of factor input was the same in the production of all broad types of final product. I shall illustrate the procedure by estimating the change from 1929 to 1972 for nondurable goods. Data are based on 1972 price weights, which BEA used until its 1986 revision, because I have previously calculated output per unit of input on the basis of these weights but not of the 1982 weights that BEA now uses.

The 1972 index of nonresidential business sector national income in current prices was 1,019.5 when 1929 equals 100; this is an index of the total cost of employing the factors of production in the sector. The 1972 index of the quantity of factor inputs (1929 = 100) in the sector was 177.7.[14] For the sector as a whole, the 1972 price index of a composite unit of factor input (1929 = 100) was therefore 1,019.5/177.7, or 573.7.

I now introduce the assumption that the percentage change in the price of a composite unit of factor input was the same for the produc-

13. It may be noted that René Durand and Mehrzad Salem of Statistics Canada are exploring estimates of multifactor productivity by end product for Canada, where the task is facilitated by detailed annual input-output tables.

14. Computed from Edward F. Denison, *Trends in American Economic Growth, 1929–1982* (Brookings, 1985), tables 2-5 and 4-6, col. 9.

tion of nondurable goods as for nonresidential business as a whole. It would be correct if a unit of factor input (allowing for quality differences) earned the same amount anywhere within nonresidential business in 1929 and also in 1972. It would also be correct even if there were differences in earnings in 1929 if they persisted to 1972.

But this assumption is hazardous for short-period comparisons. Because some prices lag behind others, it is risky even for long-period comparisons if either terminal year falls within or just after a period of sharp change in the general price level. Without close investigation it is also hazardous under most conditions for an individual product, whose price at any particular date may be affected by special influences.

The comparison to be made in this illustration, of nondurable goods with all nonresidential business output, focuses on broad composites. The years compared are far apart. The year 1929 followed several years of only moderate movements of general prices, and 1972 followed several years of price increases that, though appreciable, were not highly concentrated and were much smaller than in later years.

The 1972 index of the current-price value of expenditure for nondurable goods was 816.3 (1929 = 100).[15] Dividing by 573.7, the price index for factor inputs, yields 142.3 as the index of the quantity of inputs entering into nondurable goods.

The 1972 index of the value in constant (1972) prices of the output of nondurable goods was 314.2 (1929 = 100).[16] Dividing by 142.3, the index of the quantity of inputs, yields 220.8 as the index of output per unit of input. Thus output per unit of input in the production and distribution of nondurable goods increased 120.8 percent from 1929 to 1972 as against an increase of 100.5 percent for all the output of nonresidential business.[17] The 1929–72 annual growth rate for nondurable goods was 1.86 percent, compared with 1.63 percent for the entire nonresidential business sector.

A less obvious method that yields the same result uses no informa-

15. U.S. Bureau of Economic Analysis, *The National Income and Product Accounts of the United States, 1929–76: Statistical Tables* (Department of Commerce, 1981), table 1.3. This source is used for comparability with the other data used in the illustration.

16. Ibid., table 1.4.

17. Denison, *Trends in American Economic Growth, 1929–1982*, table 4-6, col. 11.

TABLE 4-1. *Growth Rates of Implicit Price Deflators and Differences in Implied Growth Rates of Output per Unit of Input for Gross Domestic Business Product and Its Final Product Components, 1929–86*[a]

Item	1929–86	1929–48	1948–73	1973–86	1973–79	1979–86	1979–82	1982–86
	GROWTH RATES OF IMPLICIT PRICE DEFLATORS (PERCENT A YEAR)							
GDBP, total	3.50	2.59	2.68	6.47	8.05	5.14	8.36	2.78
Housing services	2.87	0.04	3.08	6.74	7.13	6.41	9.48	4.16
GDBP except housing services	3.56	2.84	2.64	6.44	8.13	5.02	8.27	2.64
Goods and structures	3.38	2.80	2.47	6.04	8.12	4.29	7.50	1.94
Goods	3.18	2.48	2.37	5.80	7.54	4.32	7.45	2.04
Durable	3.12	2.29	2.21	6.15	7.52	4.99	9.06	2.04
Nondurable	3.20	2.56	2.48	5.56	7.66	3.79	6.15	2.06
Structures	4.18	3.64	3.04	6.90	10.21	4.15	7.77	1.52
Services except housing	4.11	2.65	3.45	7.38	8.27	6.63	10.11	4.09
	DIFFERENCES IN GROWTH RATES OF OUTPUT PER UNIT OF INPUT IMPLIED BY PRICES (PERCENTAGE POINTS)[b]							
GDBP, total	0.06	0.25	−0.04	−0.03	0.13	−0.12	−0.09	−0.14
Housing services	0.69	2.80	−0.44	−0.30	1.00	−1.39	−1.21	−1.52
GDBP except housing services	0.00	0.00	0.00	0.00	0.00	0.00	0.00	0.00
Goods and structures	0.18	0.04	0.17	0.40	0.01	0.73	0.77	0.70
Goods	0.38	0.36	0.27	0.64	0.59	0.70	0.82	0.60
Durable	0.44	0.55	0.43	0.29	0.61	0.03	−0.79	0.60
Nondurable	0.36	0.28	0.16	0.88	0.47	1.23	2.12	0.58
Structures	−0.62	−0.80	−0.40	−0.54	−2.08	0.87	0.50	1.12
Services except housing	−0.55	0.19	−0.81	−0.94	−0.14	−1.61	−1.84	−1.45

SOURCES: Author's calculations using U.S. Bureau of Economic Analysis, *The National Income and Product Accounts of the United States, 1929–82: Statistical Tables* (Department of Commerce, 1986), tables 1.23, 1.24, 1.3, 1.4, 1.7, 1.8, 7.5, and 7.6; and *Survey of Current Business*, vol. 67 (July 1987), same tables.

a. Data adjusted to exclude exceptional quality improvement in computers, as explained in chapter 2.

b. Excess over rate for GDBP except housing services.

tion about components except relative price movements. In 1972 the implicit price deflator for nondurable goods was 259.7 (1929 = 100); that for nonresidential business national income was 286.2.[18] The ratio of the first index number to the second is 0.908. Dividing the index of output per unit of input for nonresidential business, 200.5, by this ratio yields 220.8, the same index of output per unit of input in the production and distribution of nondurable goods as before.

These calculations cannot be updated to the present because neither output in 1972 prices nor my series for output per unit of input is available. But by switching to 1982 prices, one can calculate *differences* between growth rates of prices and (by inference) differences among growth rates of gross output per unit of input.

The upper half of table 4-1 shows the growth rates of implicit price deflators for gross domestic business product (GDBP) and its major components, by type of product, for selected periods. GDBP includes services of both owner-occupied and tenant-occupied housing. The bottom half shows the implied amount by which the growth rate of output per unit of input for each component exceeds the rate for GDBP except housing services. To illustrate, from 1929 to 1986 the growth rate of prices of goods and structures was 0.18 percentage point below that of GDBP except housing services, so it is inferred that the growth rate of output per unit of input was 0.18 percentage point higher.

Table 4-1 is calculated on a GNP basis, like the BLS industry series. Housing services, though shown, are excluded from the series for business GNP that is used as a standard of comparison with components.[19] There are two reasons for this. First, because of their unusual input composition, housing services are usually treated separately in analyzing productivity growth. Second, as I have explained elsewhere, the series for the constant-dollar value of the stock of housing is unlikely to be statistically consistent with the series for the constant-dollar value of housing services, so that changes in output per unit of input in this sector are highly suspect, whether obtained directly or by inference

18. *National Income and Product Accounts of the United States, 1929–76,* table 7.6.

19. Business except housing services in table 4-1, unlike nonresidential business as used in NIPA or my growth studies, excludes the value of intermediate goods and services used in providing housing services.

from prices.[20] Data in the table are adjusted to exclude extraordinary improvement in the quality of computers.

During the half-century from 1929 to 1979 output per unit of input grew only a little faster in the production of commodities (goods and structures) than in the production of all business products except housing (table 4-1). The difference in growth rates was only 0.04 percentage point in 1929–48, 0.17 point in 1948–73, and 0.01 point in 1973–79. It jumped abruptly to 0.73 percentage point in 1979–86 (0.77 point in 1979–82 and 0.70 point in 1982–86).

Within this commodity aggregate, the growth rate of output per unit of input in producing structures was below the sector rate until 1979; the gap was 0.40 to 0.80 percentage point until 1973, then jumped to 2.08 points in 1973–79. The difference was reversed in 1979–86, when the performance of structures bettered that of the sector by 0.50 percentage point in 1979–82 and 1.12 points in 1982–86. The wide short-period fluctuations after 1973 may reflect leads and lags in prices, for from 1973 to 1986 as a whole output per unit of input for structures grew at a rate of 0.54 percentage point less than in the sector, not very different from the 1929–73 experience.

For goods, the implied growth rate of output per unit of input in 1929–48 and 1948–73 was 0.3 or 0.4 percentage point above the rate for all business product except housing services. Thereafter the difference was wider, 0.6 to 0.8 percentage point. Although the difference was fairly steady for goods as a whole in the period from 1979 to 1986, that was not true for durable and nondurable goods separately. The difference for durables swung from 0.6 percentage point in 1973–79 to −0.8 point in 1979–82 and back to 0.6 point in 1982–86. Meanwhile the difference for nondurables jumped from 0.5 percentage point in 1973–79 to 2.1 points in 1979–82, then fell back to 0.6 point in 1982–86.

There are huge differences in scope and concept between output per unit of input for durable and nondurable goods in table 4-1 and output per hour in durable and nondurable goods manufacturing in table 3-1. It is therefore not surprising that growth rate differences for these series

20. See, for example, Edward F. Denison, *Accounting for United States Economic Growth, 1929–1969* (Brookings, 1974), pp. 170–80, and *Accounting for Slower Economic Growth: The United States in the 1970s* (Brookings, 1979), pp. 88–90.

are, in general, very different. After 1979, however, there is one striking similarity. In both tables the excess of productivity growth in durables over that in the business sector was negative in 1979–82 and extraordinarily large in 1982–86, whereas in nondurable goods the excess was huge in 1979–82 and much lower in 1982–86. The similarity may lend credence to this strange pattern. In contrast, for the whole 1973–86 period of productivity slowdown, the final product estimates show the growth rate for nondurable goods to have been a substantial 0.6 percentage point above that for durables, whereas the industry data in table 3-1 show the growth rate to have been 0.2 point higher in durable than in nondurable goods manufacturing.

In production of services except housing, output per unit of input grew about as much from 1929 to 1948 and again from 1973 to 1979 as it did in production of all GDBP except housing. But from 1948 to 1973 the growth rate for services was lower by 0.8 percentage point and from 1979 to 1986 by 1.6 points. Service prices lagged behind commodity prices during and just after World War II, which tended to cause overstatement of the productivity increase inferred for services in 1929–48 and understatement in 1948–73. Over the 1973–86 productivity slowdown period as a whole, the services shortfall from the sector growth rate was only slightly larger than in 1948–73, according to these calculations.

The constant-dollar value of services except housing has consistently been much smaller than that of goods and structures. In the terminal years of the periods shown in table 4-1, it has fluctuated from 36 percent of the value of goods and structures in 1929 down to 27 percent in 1953, up to 49 percent in 1982, and back to 47 percent in 1986.[21] Because of their smaller size, services normally differ from the sector growth rate much more than commodities do. The sector rate, however, is not simply a weighted average of the rates for the two components; it can be appreciably affected by changes in weights.

As emphasized earlier, one can rely more on indirect estimates of output per unit of factor input for long periods than for short ones, and rapid changes in prices reduce their reliability regardless of the length

21. Author's calculations using *National Income and Product Accounts of the United States, 1929–82*, and *Survey of Current Business*, vol. 67 (July 1987), tables 1.24, 1.4, 1.8.

of the period. Indirect estimates provide the best evidence now available on differential changes in output per unit of factor input by end product categories, but they do not eliminate the need for direct estimates of output per unit of input, multifactor productivity, and eventually output per unit of factor input.

Concluding Comment

Criticisms of estimates of output, and hence of productivity, by industry do not apply to productivity estimates for the business sector as a whole. Estimates of productivity for the sector are not obtained by combining estimates by industry; they are obtained independently and make no use of industry data for output. On the contrary, estimates of output by industry—and hence of output per hour and multifactor productivity by industry—are obtained by dividing sector output totals among industries.[22] It is to this process that my concerns about statistical accuracy and conceptual meaning pertain. I regard annual productivity series for the business sector as reasonably satisfactory, apart from the handling of computers.

Because of the partitioning procedure described, it is untenable to argue, as some do, that manufacturing data are reliable and nonmanufacturing data are not. Given that industry data result from dividing of a known total, if the increase in nonmanufacturing output is understated by one dollar, the increase in manufacturing output is overstated by one dollar. The fact that manufacturing is little more than one-third as big as nonmanufacturing means that if nonmanufacturing productivity growth were understated by 1 percentage point, manufacturing productivity growth would be overstated by nearly 3 percentage points.

22. Apart from the minor "residual" entry.

INDEX

Advances in knowledge, contribution to growth, 10, 13, 24, 25, 62; distinguished from capital contributions, 30–32; origin of, 63; understatement of, 30–32

Agriculture
- Employment, 53
- Productivity, 41; constant in agricultural services, 52; reduction of excess labor and, 63; vertical disintegration and overstatement of in farming, 53–54

Alterman, Jack, 66

Baily, Martin Neil, 35n

BEA. *See* Bureau of Economic Analysis

BLS. *See* Bureau of Labor Statistics

Bureau of Economic Analysis (BEA), 2
- Capital input measure, 25
- GNP estimates by final product, 64–65
- GNP estimates by industry, 7, 8, 39; evaluation of, 12–13; implicit deflators for, 17–18; inconsistencies between BLS employment data and, 56–58; industries estimated by constant labor productivity, 43–44, 51–52; industries estimated by double deflation, 42–43, 44–49; industries estimated by single deflation, 43, 49–51
- Input-output tables, 65–66
- National income and product accounts, 67
- New computer price index, 15, 24, 27; capital stock estimates, 28, 29, 31

Bureau of Labor Statistics (BLS), 2
- Capital input measure, 23, 25
- Employment and hours data, 39, 56–58, 66, 67
- Multifactor productivity series, 1, 2, 5
- Output per hour series, 1, 2; for commodity-producing versus service industries, 6; compared with Denison series, 5; data for, 15, 16; by industry, 10–11, 39; valuation of computer production in, 8–10, 15

Business cycle, effect on productivity, 11–12, 41–42

Business sector, scope, 1n, 5–6

Capital input
- Computer production, 8, 16, 19: contribution to growth, 31–32; quality changes effect on, 17, 25–26, 27, 36; timing of productivity increase and, 32–35
- Contribution to growth, 23, 24, 25, 31
- Measures of, 10, 23
- *See also* Capital stock

Capital stock
- Advances in knowledge and contribution to, 30–31
- Computer share of business, 23
- Measurement of quality changes in: by capital input-output ratio, 27–28; by consumption forgone, 30–32; by cost, 26–27; by marginal products, 28–30

Cartright, David W., 15n

Cas, Alexandra, 32n

Census Bureau, 26

Chakrabarti, Alok K., 35n

Cole, Rosanne, 15n

Commodity-producing industries, 6
- Productivity growth estimates, 12, 13; by double deflation, 42–43, 44–49, 52; by single deflation, 43, 49–51; vertical disintegration and overestimation of, 52–55
- Share of nonresidential GNP, 60–61

Competition. *See* Foreign competition

Computer production
- Contribution to growth by quality changes in computers, 8, 16, 17, 19, 25, 27, 36

Productivity, 1; design components and, 8, 15; effect on business sector output, 19–22; methods for measuring 35, 36–37; overstatement of, 8, 17–18, 24; slowdown in, 17, 35
Computer-using industries, effect of computers on productivity growth in, 9, 16, 17, 32–35
Constant-labor-productivity industries, GNP estimates, 12, 43–44, 51–52
Contributions to growth
Advances in knowledge, 10, 25, 31–32
Capital input, 23, 24, 25, 31
Classification of sources, 24–25

Dean, Edwin, 2n, 64n
de Leeuw, Frank, 7n, 29n
Denison, Edward F., 4n, 18n, 24n, 26n, 30n, 31n, 34n, 36n, 68n, 69n
Double deflation
Defined, 12
GNP estimates by, 42–43: criteria for using, 45; inconsistency in data for, 44–46; statistical weakness of, 46–48
Durand, René, 32n, 68n

Employment
Agricultural, 53
BLS series, 56–58
By end product, 66–67
Service industries, 54

Factor inputs
Classification by end product, 14, 61; direct estimation, 65; flexibility in, 67; indirect estimation, 68–71
Classification by industry, 61
Computer measurement and growth rate of, 17–18, 23, 29
Index of quantity of, 68–69
Foreign competition, effect on productivity in durable goods manufacturing, 11–12, 59
Foss, Murray F., 31n

GNP. *See* Gross national product
Government enterprises, 5
Output per hour, 41
Griliches, Zvi, 26n
Gross domestic business product, growth rate, 71
Gross national product (GNP)
Constant-labor-productivity industries, 43–44, 51–52
Estimates, by final product, 64–65
Growth: computer production improvements and, 9–10, 16–19, 22, 24; NNP growth and, 21–22; overstatement of, 8–10, 22, 24
Measurement, by industry, 2, 7, 39, 42–56
Gullickson, William, 39n

Harper, Michael J., 39n
Harrod-Robinson-Read measure of capital, 30n
Hicks-Meade-Solow measure of capital, 30n
Hill, T. P., 44–45, 50n
Hours of work, BLS data, 2, 39, 56–58
Housing services, in productivity growth analysis, 71–72

Input-output, BEA data, 65–66, 67
Inventories
BEA data, 66, 67
Contribution to national income growth rate, 31

Jaszi, George, 26n

Kunze, Kent, 2n

Labor input
BEA versus BLS estimates, 56–58
By end product, 65, 68
In multifactor productivity, 5
Quality adjustment of, 6

Manufacturing industries, 1
Multifactor productivity, 5–6
Output per hour growth rate: changes in, 2–4, 10–11; cyclical effects on, 11–12; data reliability for, 6–7, 8–9, 10–13, 19, 39–59; double deflation to measure, 45–47; durables versus nondurables, 11–12, 41–42; foreign competition and, 11–12
Marginal productivity theory, 36–37
Mark, Jerome A., 51n
Mishel, Lawrence, 7n
Multifactor productivity
BLS series, 1, 2, 5

Classified by end product, 67–68
Computer use and, 32–33
Defined, 5
Factor inputs to derive, 65
Weights in measuring, 23, 33–34

National income and products accounts (NIPA), 2, 67
Neef, Arthur, 64n
Net national product (NNP), 6
Computer productivity effect on growth rate of, 16; through computer replacement, 33–34; for manufacturing versus nonmanufacturing, 21–22, 23
Estimates by end product, 64–65
Overstatement of growth, 8–9
NIPA. *See* National income and product accounts
NNP. *See* Net national product
Nonmanufacturing industries
Output per hour growth rate: changes in, 1–4, 8, 10–11; computer production and, 19–20; methodology and data reliability for, 6–7, 39–59
Nonresidential business sector
GNP, by end product, 60, 67
Index of composite unit of factor inputs, 68–69
National income in current prices, 68
Net output per hour, 4n, 5
Output per unit of input, 6

Output per hour, by end product, 2, 13–14
Distinguished from output per hour, by industry, 60–61
Estimation of, 64–68
Output per hour, by industry, 7
Computer production productivity and, 8, 16, 19–20
Conceptual problems, 61–64
Data deficiencies in, 2, 12–13, 14, 39–59, 61–62
Durable versus nondurable manufacturing industries, 41–42
Growth rate, 2, 4, 39–42; cyclical effects on, 11–12, 41; foreign competition effects on, 11–12, 59
Manufacturing versus nonmanufacturing industries, 1–4, 8, 10–11, 19–20, 58–59
Methods of estimating changes in: adjustments in data consistency to improve, 55–56; constant productivity assumption for, 51–52; double deflation, 42–43, 44–49, 53; hours of work data for, 56–58; single deflation, 43, 49–51, 53
Sources of error: inadequate information, 44–59; overweighting, and concept of, computer prices, 8–10, 15–38
Output per unit of input, by end product
Direct estimates, 14, 65–68
Growth rates: for durable versus nondurable goods, 69–71, 72–73; for goods versus services, 72–73; for gross domestic business product, 71; input measures for, 68
Indirect estimates based on price movements, 68–73; reliability, 73–74
Output per unit of input, by industry
Advances in knowledge as source of, 10, 16, 62, 63
Business sector versus individual industries, 63
Computer production contribution to growth, 15–17, 19–20; by computer replacement, 32–35; methods for measuring, 35–37; by quality changes in computers, 25, 27, 35, 36
Conceptual aspects, 61–64
Market size contribution to growth, 63

Pasinetti, Luigi L., 36–37
Production function, 31–32n
Productivity. *See* Multifactor productivity; Output per hour, by end product; Output per hour, by industry; Output per unit of input, by end product; Output per unit of input, by industry

Research and development, and productivity change, 62–63
Resource allocation, and productivity change, 13, 63
Retail trade, output per hour growth rate, 41
Rymes, Thomas K., 30, 32n

Salem, Mehrzad, 32n, 68n
Service industries, 6
GNP estimates, 13–14, 60

Prices, versus commodity prices, 47
Productivity growth estimates: by constant-productivity assumption, 52, 54; by single deflation, 49
Value of GNP, 60–61
SIC. *See* Standard industrial classification
Single deflation, 12
To estimate GNP, 43
Industries estimated by, 49
Problems relating to, 50–52
Standard industrial classification (SIC), 39n; 66, 67

Technological improvements, contribution to productivity growth, 13, 63
Triplett, Jack E., 31n, 37n

Underground economy adjustment, 56–57

Vertical disintegration, and errors in estimates of productivity growth by industry, 52–55

Wholesale trade, output per hour growth rate, 41